LIFE STRATEGIES FROM A LIFE COACH

THE KEYS TO A REMARKABLE LIFE

LOURENS BOTHA

Published by MyLife
1st Floor Block B, Trent Bridge Office Park
Corner of Von Willich Ave & Leonie Street, Centurion, South Africa
www.mylife.co.za

Copyright © 2020 Lourens Botha

All rights reserved.
No part of this book may be reproduced or transmitted in any form or by any means, electronic or mechanical, including photocopying, recording, or by any information storage and retrieval system, without permission in writing from the publisher.

Proofreading: Dr. Gerhard Bothma
Layout: Christina van Straaten
Book cover: Anja Richards

Printed and bound by Ingram Spark

First published 2020
First print 2020

ISBN: 978-0-6398358-8-4

Table of Contents

FOREWORD i

INTRODUCTION iii

PART 1: PLAN YOUR JOURNEY 1

   YOU NEED MORE THAN TALENT 2
   PLAN THE JOURNEY TO YOUR GOALS 6
   BECOME A BETTER VERSION OF YOURSELF 8
   UNLEASH YOUR CREATIVITY 11
   FIND YOUR INNER-ADVENTURER 14
   START WITH THE RESULT 18
   PAY THE RIGHT PRICE FOR YOUR GOALS 21
   PUT YOUR DREAMS TO WORK 24

PART 2: LIVE WITH IMPACT 27

   START CONSISTENTLY SMALL 28
   LIVE A LIFE OF IMPACT 32
   TELL YOUR STORY 35
   CULTIVATE A FORWARD REACHING MINDSET 38
   FIND THE COURAGE TO CONTINUE 41
   GIVE YOURSELF TIME TO HEAL 44
   FIND MEANING IN THE CONTRASTS OF LIFE 47
   EMIGRATE YOUR MIND 50
   FIND YOUR MOUNTAIN MAGIC 53
   BE THE ESCAPE ROUTE 56
   ROLL WITH THE PUNCHES OF LIFE 59
   BECOME A FACILITATOR FOR SUCCESS 62

PART 3: HAVE A MIRACLE MINDSET 67
FIND YOUR RECIPE TO BOUNCE BACK AFTER ADVERSITY ... 68
VALUE YOUR TIME... 71
LEAD BY EXAMPLE 74
WIN THE BATTLE BETWEEN COMFORT AND WILLPOWER ... 78
DISCOVER YOUR POTENTIAL 81
CHASE YOUR GOALS 85
THE ART OF LETTING GO 88
ENRICH YOUR LIFE WITH GREAT PEOPLE................................ 92
FIND A DEEPER AWARENESS FOR YOUR WORLD..................... 95

PART 4: WRITE AN EXTRAORDINARY STORY 99
CULTIVATE YOUR OWN HAPPINESS... 100
DEVELOP THE LEADER IN YOU 103
FIND YOUR COURAGE 106
DESIGN YOUR OPPORTUNITIES... 109
INVEST IN PEOPLE.. 113
TOGETHER WE ARE BETTER.. 116
RESOLVE CONFLICT AND FACILITATE SOLUTIONS.................. 118

PART 5: CULTIVATE YOUR HABITS 123
DESIGN HABITS FOR SUCCESS.. 124
OWN YOUR ATTITUDE... 127
FIND MEANING IN THE CHAOS 130
FIND PURPOSE IN PATIENCE... 133
CHASE SERENDIPITY.. 137

PART 6: DESIGN YOUR STRATEGY FOR LIFE 141
TAKE A CALCULATED RISK 142
GET UP ONE MORE TIME 144
CAPTAIN THE SHIP 147

ASSEMBLE YOUR INNER CIRCLE 150
UNLOCK YOUR EMOTIONAL INTELLIGENCE 154
BECOME RESILIENT 159
PREVENT BURNOUT 162
MAKE CHANGE YOUR ALLY 165
UNLOCK YOUR INFLUENCE 170
FINAL THOUGHT 173

BIBLIOGRAPHY AND PREFERRED READING 176

FOREWORD

> *" It's my life*
> *It's now or never*
> *I ain't gonna live forever*
> *I just want to live while I'm alive. "*
>
> **- Jon Bon Jovi**

Whenever I contemplate life these words from Jon Bon Jovi's Hit Song immediately come to mind and get my adrenalin pumping and my feet tapping.

I love life and LIVE my life.

Being a student of life and avid reader, I with enthusiasm devour books on the ars vivendi – the art of life. How many books, blogs and pages I've read and conversations I've had on life and living I won't be able to calculate. I've even dared to write about this great gift I – like you – have received. Loosely translated from the Afrikaans, the title of one of the books I've written is Choose Life! ... Live! Laugh! Love!

Lourens embodies this. When I met him in 2016 the first thing that struck me was how he radiated life. His laugh is contagious and his love for his family, friends and others abounds. I enjoy our conversations, his writing and musings. He informs, enlightens and inspires.

We at MyLife are therefore excited with this publication. It resonates with our endeavour to journey with people who intentionally seek sustainable emotional, social and financial health – and wealth.

Lourens in this book offers helpful keys to creating and sustaining a remarkable life. The book is written in an accessible fashion. He assists the reader to discover and live a life of significance. Just because the content reads easily does not mean it isn't sound, tried and tested. It's real. He seamlessly draws from what he has learned from experts and experienced himself and with each chapter serves us with more than a healthy meal.

Be sure to visit our platform at www.mylife.co.za and our magazine at www.mylifemag.co.za.

None of us is going to live forever. Claim your life as yours. And fully live while you're alive.

Gerhard Bothma
(Ph.D. University of Pretoria)

Editor: MyLife Magazine

INTRODUCTION

How do I find myself and purpose within the challenges, expectations and uncertainty of this life? This is the burning question in my mind. The question that never goes away, never gets fully answered and always gets me to the next question. I am probably not destined to answer this question, partly because I see my life as a journey of experience, knowledge, growth and self-actualisation. I do not see my life as an expectation or a destination. When it comes to your journey there is no right or wrong approach, timeline or progress. What is of importance is that we stay aware of the journey, stay aware of the fact that we are always en route and that we will never arrive. We never arrive because this journey has no destination, it only has experience. Most of what we experience results from our lack of control. If you think about it, the only variable we can control is our attitude, choices and actions. Trying to control anything outside of yourself would be a futile exercise and frankly, a waste of time and energy.

How then do I then get a grasp on life? To give my thought processes purpose and a sense of control, I have a NEVER checklist. This checklist assists me to stay true to myself and my journey. The checklist is not there to tell me where I should be, what I should have done or even what I still need to achieve. The checklist is there to keep me moving forward.

- Never see yourself as the enemy. Make peace with yourself and who you are.
- Never stop believing in yourself, your potential and your ability to impact the lives of others.

- Never compare yourself to others. Your life and your journey are unique and precious.
- Never stop caring for yourself and others.
- Never stop learning, experiencing and growing.
- Never stop celebrating. We need to enjoy the journey.
- Never be afraid to let go and try something new.
- Never exchange safety of experience.
- Never blame but rather try to understand.
- Never take life too seriously or you might lose yourself and your way.
- Never forget to forgive, so that you can travel light.
- Never travel alone. Life is not, a journey for one.
- Never leave this journey fresh. You should be exhausted and satisfied at the end, no matter how soon the end comes.

When I keep my Never-list close, I always find a sense of purpose. Whether this mindset is accurate or not, is irrelevant. This mindset keeps me moving forward and helps me to focus on my journey. The more purpose I find in my own life the more my focus moves outward and the more I can contribute to the lives around me. The opposite is unfortunately also true, the less purpose I find in my life the more my focus will be inward and the less by contribution to the lives around me.

Allow the principle in this book to get you thinking about your life, get the gears of your life moving with purpose and stimulate your excitement for this once-off journey. You don't need to remember or even practice all the principles as long as you keep some for yourself. The more you keep for yourself the more you will be able to give away, freely.

May this book lead to an inward discovery and an outward impact.

May you live and experience a remarkable life.

> *As far as we can discern, the sole purpose of human existence is to kindle a light in the darkness of mere being.*
>
> **- Carl Jung**

PART 1:

PLAN YOUR JOURNEY

YOU NEED MORE THAN TALENT

My life as a coach has shown me that if you want to become extraordinary, talent is not enough to get you there. Talent can give you a great start but will only take you so far. To become extraordinary, one needs a mind of steel, unrivalled determination, agility, adaptability, a strong support system and unstoppable resilience. You need a great strategy and a brilliant plan to execute your strategy. You need the support, guidance and advice of quality people and you need a goal that scares you. You need to understand the principle of Synergy: Together we are better. You also need to understand that the way life unfolds on your journey will not be the way you dreamed. You will need to be adaptable to counter the disappointment of life not panning out according to your expectations. You will need to be agile to capitalise on new and diverse opportunities, fast. Inflexible thinking will close doors and agility will open them.

> *" Bodybuilding is much like any other sport. To be successful, you must dedicate yourself 100% to your training, diet and mental approach. "*
>
> **- Arnold Schwarzenegger**

I have seen many talented athletes not fulfilling their potential because they were not resilient, lacked focus or were unable to adapt to change. I have seen talent go to waste because athletes did not have a strategy and plan to manage and develop themselves and their careers.

I have seen athletes fail because they lacked the basics. For me, the basics always start with the fitness of the athlete. You don't teach skills to an unfit athlete and talent is not a "Get out of jail free" card. Fitness is the key to success. In any facet of life, we need to train hard to become the best we can be. We need to be fit for life before we can excel in life.

Why are so many of our athletes not fit enough, then? They probably hate laying the groundwork. They are not willing to pay the price that comes with the goal. They are not committed. Committed to endless hours spent in the gym or exhausting fitness sessions. They are not committed to spending hour upon hour working on developing a robust strategy and a plan to get them to their goals.

It is a lot more fun to practice skills and play a game than it is to train. Not to mention the effort it takes to stay fit and in top shape. If you want to get fit and stay fit, you need one thing: Consistency. Fitness is a lifestyle and not a skill. By working on your fitness, you are laying the groundwork for your success. You don't need to be the most talented, but you have to be the most committed. Work on your game off the field so that your talent can shine on the field. Do the hard work behind the scenes so that you can make it look easy on the field.

> *" Practice puts brains in your muscles. "*
>
> **- Sam Snead**

Your talent is the headings in the story of your life, but your fitness and commitment are the stories below those headings. Your headings will be read and soon forgotten, but your stories will remain in the hearts of people. Those hours on the road, in the pool, on the bike or in the gym, are the times when you are writing your story. It is those times that make your story and allow you to shine in the arena.

This principle is applicable everywhere in life. Opportunities and success are the headings of our story, but our stories are told by consistency, hard work and perseverance. Just like an athlete, you also need a strong mind to keep fit for life. Your mental toughness will help you to be consistent and keep you going when times are tough. It will help you to keep on building quality habits and developing yourself into a better version of yourself. It will help you get up after you fall and it will be the motivator that drags you across the finish line.

Before you get excited about your talent, make sure you lay the groundwork and do the basics well, so that your talent can speak for itself.

> *" The price of success is hard work, dedication to the job at hand, and the determination that whether we win or lose, we have applied the best of ourselves to the task at hand. "*
>
> **- Vince Lombardi**

12 Elements to make your talent shine:
1. Determination and Commitment to prevent you from giving up.
2. Resilience to carry you when the odds are against you.

3. Adaptability to keep you from getting stuck behind expectations.
4. Agility to help you capitalise on the next opportunity coming your way.
5. Consistency so that you can be effective and reach your goals.
6. A support structure to pick you up and keep you going.
7. Vision to know where you need to be.
8. Goals to help you understand what you need to do while you here.
9. Plans to get you to your goals.
10. Strategy to help you become extraordinary not only in a goal but in life.
11. Synergy so that you don't travel alone.
12. Energy so that you can get up even when you don't want to.

Final thought: If you want to be the best, you need to be willing to endure more pain than the next person. You need to be willing to pay a higher price. Success is an expensive and rare commodity. Your success is defined by you.

> *Physical fitness is extremely important to me. Only if you are fit will you be able to achieve whatever you want to achieve in life; you will be able to pursue your dreams, your ambition, your goals, and the things you love.*
>
> **- Urvashi Rautela**

PLAN THE JOURNEY TO YOUR GOALS

If you want to get to a new place in your life you will have to take the first step and act. Like an athlete that has to go for a run, the first step is always the most difficult. Most of the time, putting on your running shoes on a cold winter's morning will be the most difficult part of the run. You need to know where you want to go and what you want to achieve. If you know what you want to achieve, you will need a plan to get there. Without a plan, you will remain trapped in your comfort zone and live your life as a dreamer.

> *A dream gives us direction, but a plan gets us moving.*
>
> **– Lourens Botha**

Planning your journey is not just another step in the process, it is a large part of achieving your goal.

Seven advantages of planning how to achieve your goals:

1. It allows us to visit and evaluate our goals in a structured way. It takes us through the logical steps needed to achieve our goals.
2. It helps us to identify some of the pitfalls we will experience along the way.
3. It gives us the opportunity to spend time with our dreams and therefore helps us to keep our dreams alive.

4. It allows us to interact with people. It helps us to network, meet new people and gain new insight into the process.

5. By planning to reach your goals you take accountability for our dreams and make sure you set the ball in motion to achieve them.

6. Planning our goals motivates the people around us and set them on their way to achieving their goals. Our example can change the lives of others.

7. Planning helps us to rewire our brains into an Action and Solution mode. We become "Achieving-orientated".

Final thought: We need to make sure we draw a map that will help us get to our goals but we must also ensure that our map has more than one route to get there.

> " *Stop setting goals. Goals are pure fantasy Unless you have a specific plan to achieve them.* "
>
> **- Stephen Covey**

BECOME A BETTER VERSION OF YOURSELF

Rachel Hollis nailed it when she said: *"It's not about the goal or the dream you have. It's about who you become on your way to the goal."*

Our journey through life is not about how many times we succeed or which goals we achieve. Our lives are about becoming. It's about our victory over the old version of me by the new version of me: to become a better version of myself. We are always en route, experiencing, growing, and becoming. At our core, we are travellers. We are travellers through time, always en route to the next experience.

Change is inevitable on our journey. Change is not the enemy on your journey, the enemy is the status quo and the resistance to experience life to the fullest. The mere fact that you are not growing and evolving should sound the alarm bells of your growth clock.

10 Tips for your journey of self-discovery and growth:

1. Travel lite – We carry a lot of baggage in the form of unresolved issues, fear and regrets. You need to set yourself free and only you know how to do it. You know what is holding you back and what you need to let go. You cannot change the past, but you can learn from it. You can grow, adapt and become a better version of yourself. Leave the past where it belongs: in the past. Prove yourself that you are worth more, that you can be more, and that the best of you is yet to come.

2. Celebrate regularly – Life should be a celebration. Don't wait for the big moment or big achievements before you celebrate. Find reasons to celebrate, there are enough.

3. Find the moment – Don't wait for life to give you moments to enjoy, go out and find them, plan them and set them up. This mindset will push you into motion to find quality and joy in your life. Find the things that you love and spend more time on them.

4. Dress up – Take care of yourself. Exercise, eat healthily, make time to relax and dress up. Be proud of who you are and the way you look. All these things will help you put a positive spin on life.

5. Be creative – Make sure that you give yourself time to be creative each day. You need your creativity to live a colourful life. Your creativity is what will help you discover the beautiful things in life.

6. Give – Give something for free. It can be small, as long as you give from your heart.

7. Love what you do – If you hate what you do you will be forced into a coping mindset. You will not find joy and you will lose your creativity and spontaneity. You will be in a survival mindset. If you are in a survival mindset it is probably time for you to re-evaluate your life. Time to change what you do, the way you do it or even the way you look at it.

8. Talk – Have at least one meaningful conversation per day. Talk and listen to find new insights and discover new ways of looking at life. Talk to an audience of diverse people, people who look at life from a different perspective.

9. Laugh – Be the one who laughs the loudest. Remember that laughing is addictive, you will draw a crowd.

10. Love them – Tell them that you love them. Make sure they know it and that it is more than just words.

Final thought: The smart thing to do is to use your time wisely and make sure you enjoy the journey and not live for the goal.

> *Do the one thing you think you cannot do.*
> *Fail at it. Try again. Do better the second time.*
> *The only people who never tumble are those*
> *who never mount the high wire.*
> *This is your moment. Own it.*
>
> **- Oprah Winfrey**

UNLEASH YOUR CREATIVITY

You are a unique human being; you have your specific place in the puzzle of life. Your puzzle piece is unique and can only fit in one opening and in one way. Your uniqueness completes the puzzle of life and helps those around you to make sense of the world. Without you, those around you will not see the full picture of life. You are gifted with your uniqueness and creativity and it is your mandate to make the world a better place with those gifts.

> " *Your life is your canvas, and you are the masterpiece. There are a million ways to be kind, amazing, fabulous, creative, bold, and interesting.* "
>
> **- Kerli**

What will set you apart in a world where more and more people are doing the same thing, where more and more organizations are supplying the same product or service? Your creativity will give you the edge. It will make you rise head and shoulders above the rest. How do we develop our creativity? Start by building a strategy around the following areas:

1. **Create a creativity space** – Successful companies like Zappo's allow their people to create their workspace. This means that their people work in an environment that is visually conducive to creativity. What type of environment will stimulate your creativity?

2. **Use your creativity window** – Your creativity will not be at the same level all day long. You have a window period of a couple of

hours where your creativity will be at its highest. Identify your window and use it to your advantage.

3. **Take regular breaks** – Working nonstop kills creativity. Tired, overworked and overstressed people cannot be creative. Allow yourself enough breaks so that your body and mind can recover and your inspiration can return.

4. **Get a diverse opinion** – Make sure you speak to people who see the world from a different perspective. People who will challenge your "traditional" believes. Being forced to look at life from a different perspective unleashes our creativity and opens all kinds of new possibilities.

5. **Take risks** – Creativity and risk go hand in hand. Don't expect yourself or someone else to be creative without taking risks. Creativity is a risky business because you play where no one else has played before. You make mistakes and start over until you come up with something unique and authentic. You need to colour outside the lines and play outside the box. Only if you are willing to open yourself to criticism and failure, can you truly operate outside the traditional boundaries and be creative.

6. **Be curious and ask questions** – We ask fewer questions even though we have a treasure trove of knowledge around us. We accept what is fed to us through the media and social media. We need to question more and dig deeper to get to a better understanding. We need to take the responsibility to get to the source, ourselves. We need to make up our minds.

7. **Embracing serendipity** – For me, serendipity means: in the end, everything will work out for the best. If you take the risk and fear out of your creativity vocabulary, then you free yourself to

be creative. You give yourself breathing space to be creative and discover without the fear of consequences.

8. **Be spontaneous** – We get impulsive spurts of creativity. Make sure you capitalize on those moments. If you get an idea or insight, write it down. If you need to draw or paint, then do it. If you need to compose there and then, do it. If you don't, something valuable close to your being will be lost. If you get stuck, go and do something else, something spontaneous. If your team can't get around that problem, go and sit in a cafe, drink some coffee and have some cake. The change might just get you where you need to be. The principle is: Stop running into the same wall, turn around and take a different direction, a different approach. Try something new, something different, something fresh.

9. **Be persistent** – Creativity is a process and not an onetime event. Being creative also means that we keep on failing until we get it right. If we understand that failure is part of creativity, then we lower the value of failure and increase the value of risk. We become eager to take risks to get to an extraordinary result.

Final thought: Colour the world with your uniqueness. Make the world a colourful and bright place for those around you. Show people that their uniqueness and creativity add flavour to life.

> *To raise new questions, new possibilities, to regard old problems from a new angle, requires creative imagination and marks real advance in science.*
>
> **- Albert Einstein**

FIND YOUR INNER-ADVENTURER

Did life not turn out the way you thought it would? Do you feel unfulfilled? Are other people living the life you dreamed of? Are your friends doing the things you wanted to experience? Is there a bit of envy and regret crying inside you?

If you answered "yes" to any or all these questions, there are three things you should know:

1. You are not the only one.
2. You are ready for change.
3. You are seeing what everyone else is doing because you don't focus on your happiness.

> *All our dreams can come true if we have the courage to pursue them.*
>
> **- Walt Disney**

If we do the things that we love, those things that energize and inspire us, then we stop looking *outward* to be envious of what other people are doing. We look *inward* because we are focused on our lives and our unique journey. Where is your focus; inward or outward?

The good news is all is not lost. This, however, is not one of those over the top, Climb-Everest-and-Swim-with-Piranhas, type of book. This is a baby-step kind of book. Let's rather start with small steps and increase our appetite for adventure before we get to the big leaps. Like most things in life, an appetite for adventure can be developed by making small changes in your daily routine and habits. When I climbed Mt. Kilimanjaro some years ago, my guide told me to "Pole Pole", which in Swahili means: to take it slow. Slow, is what gets us there and what helps us to enjoy the journey and not only the destination.

One of the primary reasons people give up on their dreams is because they try to achieve too much too fast. They bite off a chunk that is too large and they become despondent. There are a few people out there that can get away with radical changes but the rest of us need to start slow, to get into the rhythm. We need to enjoy what we do while we are doing it or else our adventure will become our nightmare.

10 Steps to help you discover and activate your Inner-Adventurer (Pole Pole):

1. **Discover the day** – Be aware of what is happening in the world around you. Start to look for opportunities and new things to do. Little things also count!

2. **Break the routine** – Change your daily routine. Even if you just scramble the routine of one day a week, you will discover that by looking at a day from a different perspective, new opportunities and possibilities, appear.

3. **Have a fun-day** – Take one day in a week and design a fun-day. A day where you do things that you like. Make it special for you, a custom made "you-day". Fit it in between your daily schedule. Make it work because you want to.

4. **Be spontaneous** – Do something different and impulsive. Take yourself out of your current environment and "land" somewhere else. Experience a different moment.

5. **Say "Yes"** – You cannot change your habits, routine or life if you say "no" to everything. Start by saying "Yes". Get out, see new things, meet new people and experience life differently. People are always the keys to your next adventure.

6. **Dream big** – Don't be afraid to dream big. Dreams inspire us and take us to the life we want to have. Use the energy and momentum of your dreams to keep moving towards them. Know that worthwhile dreams need effort and commitment. You will not achieve them in a day and that is fine. Keep dreaming and keep moving.

7. **Make your list** – Make a list of 10 items that you want to do within the next 3 months. Make a list of 10 things you want to do before the next 12 months have gone by.

8. **Find new people** – People are the keys to adventure. Make it one of your priorities to meet more people and to spend more time with the people you know.

9. **Live your stories** – Make sure that the things you do fit in with the story you want to tell about your life. Do things that you will be excited to write about. Then, write your story in your own words.

10. **Take a risk** – Do something that scares you. Something that takes you out of your comfort zone. Experience the feeling of unease and excitement. Feel the adrenaline.

Final thought: A life of adventure can only be lived outside your comfort zone.

PART 1: PLAN YOUR JOURNEY

> *The biggest adventure you can take is to live the life of your dreams.*

- Oprah

START WITH THE RESULT

I love to dream about the future and the promise it holds. I love to come up with new ideas and to set new goals. Because my thinking preference is right-brain dominant, concepts like creativity, ideas and risk are all are remarkably close to my being. My biggest challenge is not coming up with new ideas or goals, my biggest challenge is to execute purposefully and maintain momentum to get to where I want to go.

If we don't understand the process that gets us to our goals and if we don't know the steps we need to take to get to our goals, most of us will barely get out of the starting blocks. The ability to get to our goals and succeed is not some secret or resides in a mystical power. The secret is in the process, knowing what the next step is and where it will take you.

Often, we have no idea what to do next and sometimes we lack courage because we are not sure what should happen next. Trying to engineer a process from start to end can leave us feeling overwhelmed. Next time you set a goal, try to reverse-engineer the result. Start by looking at the result and then ask yourself; what do I need to do to get to that result? What are the steps I need to take to get me to that result I want?

> *Success is no accident. It is hard work, perseverance, learning, studying, sacrifice and most of all, love of what you are doing or learning to do.*
>
> **- Pele**

Even if we have the steps to get to our goals, we still need a strategy to make sure we get there. This strategy should include:

- Consistency to keep us moving towards our target.
- Resilience to help us to come back from challenges, setbacks, and failure.
- Perseverance because we know why we are sacrificing to achieve this goal.

> *Success isn't always about greatness. It's about consistency. Consistent hard work leads to success. Greatness will come.*
>
> **- Dwayne Johnson**

Eight questions to understand the result you are pursuing:

1. **What will the result look like?** What will your life look like when you achieve this goal? Make sure you weigh the positives and negatives so that you understand why you are chasing this goal and know why you want to achieve it.

2. **When do I want to achieve this goal?** Timelines keep us accountable and on track.

3. **What resources do I need?** Which items should I have at my disposal if I want to succeed?

4. **Who do I need to involve?** Which people do I need and why?

5. **What level of effort will this take?** Think about time, money and energy.

6. **How many steps will it take to get there?** List all the things that it will take to get you to your goal.

7. **What should the sequence be?** Place your steps in a logical order. You have to, at all times, know what the next logical step should be.

8. **Are there any gaps?** Working backwards from the last to the first step, do your list have any gaps or big jumps between steps?

Final thought: By engineering your process to succeed, you not only give ourselves a map to get there but you also give yourself an approach that will keep you accountable and on track. You are the first and the last person that should take responsibility for your goals and success.

> *" There are no secrets to success. It is the result of preparation, hard work, and learning from failure. "*
>
> **- Colin Powell**

PAY THE RIGHT PRICE FOR YOUR GOALS

We all want to be successful, we want to achieve, excel and some of us even want to be best. We aspire to be ahead of the rest, the first to get there. Some even want to be, trendsetters and changemakers.

If we want it so bad, then why is everyone not getting there? For me, the number one reason is: Everyone is not willing to pay the price. Everything in life has a price and the only way to have a chance of receiving it or getting there, is to pay the price. We want the result, but we are not willing to pay the price.

The first two questions we should ask ourselves before attempting anything is:

- What is this going to cost me?
- Am I willing to pay the price?

> **"** *The price of success is hard work, dedication to the job at hand, and the determination that whether we win or lose, we have applied the best of ourselves to the task at hand.* **"**
>
> **- Vince Lombardi**

10 Criteria to calculate the price you are willing to pay:

1. **Physical** – How hard do I need to train? Do I need to lose weight? Do I need to change my diet? Do I need to give up exercise or sport? What needs to happen to my appearance?

2. **Emotional** – How stressful will this be? How will it affect my emotional state of mind?

3. **Relationships** – What will the impact be on my spouse, children, family, friends, colleagues and others?

4. **Spiritual** – What will the spiritual impact be? Will it help me to grow spiritually or will I recede spiritually?

5. **Financial** – Can I afford it now? What will the financial impact be, later? What will I need to give up to acquire the funds? Will I get a return on my investment? Is there a better or wiser way to spend my money? Is there a cheaper option that will still give me the same quality?

6. **Time** – How much time will this take daily, weekly and monthly? How long will this last? Do I have time to do this? Do I need to let go of something else, first? How can I make time for this?

7. **Timing** – Is this the right time to do this? When will be a better time to do this?

8. **Opportunities** – What opportunities will I lose because of this? What opportunities will I gain because of this?

9. **Long-term impact** – If I do this, what will the effect on my life be in three, five or even ten years?

10. **Legacy** – Does this fit in with the legacy I want to leave?

Final thought: Being willing to pay the price will not guarantee that you will achieve your goal, but it will help you to not pursue chasing a goal net meant for you or at least help you decide on the right timing when pursuing a goal.

> *If you believe in yourself and have dedication and pride - and never quit, you'll be a winner. The price of victory is high but so are the rewards.*
>
> **- Bear Bryant**

PUT YOUR DREAMS TO WORK

I get restless when people talk about their dreams. Maybe it's because I see the word "dream" as something that, for most people, is out of range and unachievable. I love it when people tell me what their goals are and how they are going to achieve them. I love it when people ask me to help them achieve their goals because then I know they are putting their dreams into action. I believe we should pick our dreams up from the shelf, dust them off and put them to work.

> *" Legacy is not what I did for myself. It's what I'm doing for the next generation. "*
>
> **- Vitor Belfort**

How do we put a dream to work? Well, we start by understanding why we want to live that dream, why do we want to achieve that goal? Dreams and goals need to fit into the legacy we want to leave. Our dreams need to align with the legacy we are building. If our dreams are in alignment with our legacy, we can understand why we are so passionate about them. We now have a solid foundation to come up with a strategy to chase those dreams down. I call it: a dream in action.

I believe that our passion and purpose are imprinted in our DNA and it's left there for us to discover during this wonderful journey called life. At some stage, we get to a point where we are so fed up with mediocrity in our lives that we will do almost anything to get away from it. We see our lives disappearing between the lives of the masses. We contribute to our mediocrity by keeping on accepting our lives as they are without attempting to build something unique. This is the place where you know you are a fraction of what you can be. This is the place where you know you are only scratching the surface of your potential and it is unacceptable.

This is a great place to be! At this point in your life, you have a choice to either step back into the safety of your comfort zone and be content with mediocrity, or decide to step forward into the unknown and find the life you always dreamed about. Both routes have huge implications for your life and your legacy. Whatever you decide, you need to live with the consequences.

To put your dream into action you need to understand what your passions, talents, hopes, strengths, and weaknesses are.

Eight questions to find your passion:

1. If money was not a factor, what would I do?
2. What gives excites me and gives me energy?
3. What are my talents and strengths?
4. Can I live this dream as a hobby, a career or is this just a new way of living?
5. What drains my energy and how much time do I spend doing it or being subjected to it?
6. Was there something I dreamed about as a child that still excites me?
7. How can I use my strengths and talents to put my dream in action or get to my goals?
8. Can I create something unique and relevant to my strengths and talents?

A dream in action is one of the building blocks of your legacy. The legacy that you want to leave behind to inspire people when you are not there anymore. It is also about the way we live our lives. Lives filled with courage, determination, creativity, and vision, define who we are. The pursuit of a Dream in Action is a lifelong journey, a journey filled with adventure, courage and growth.

4 Questions to understand the legacy you want to leave behind:
1. What do the life I want, look like?
2. What legacy do I want to leave behind?
3. Which three words should describe my life?
4. What do I want others to learn from my life?

Final thought: Now is the time to start hunting those dreams. Put a plan on paper. Do what you need to do to chase your dreams and goals. Leave your comfort zone behind. Get people to help you and keep you accountable so that you stay on track. Journey with people who will help you get to your goals and build a legacy.

> *So many of our dreams at first seem impossible, then they seem improbable, and then, when we summon the will, they soon become inevitable.*
>
> **– Christopher Reeve**

PART 2:

LIVE WITH IMPACT

START CONSISTENTLY SMALL

If you want to be successful, don't aim to do a great thing, do small things in a great way. Doing small things of quality, consistently, will inevitably lead to one place: success. You don't have to change the world with a fantastic performance, insight or invention. You just have to live a life of quality with consistency. By introducing quality habits into your life and consistently sticking to those habits you will not only help yourself unlock your potential, but you will also help yourself to build a life of value. It will help you to build character and discover what is possible. Even more so, it will show you what is achievable.

Consistency is the act of doing small things of quality, day in and day out, even if those things seems insignificant. Consistency is starting over when you did not previously succeed and keep going by doing the small things well. Even the smallest things done with consistency will create habits and bring extraordinary results over time. Great people do not do one great thing and then disappear, they live great lives. They are constantly learning, growing, evolving and bringing quality to a broken world. We just need to look at the life of someone like Mother Theresa, she never came up with revolutionary ideas, developed new software or designed an aircraft. She did small things day in and day out because she cared. She kept it up throughout her entire life, and today her legacy speaks for itself. Consistency, therefore, means: do the right things day in and day out, knowing that you will only see the result in future.

> *Success isn't always about greatness. It's about consistency. Consistent hard work leads to success. Greatness will come.*
>
> **- Dwayne (The Rock) Johnson**

11 Steps to cultivate consistency in your life:

1. **Understand why you are doing this** – Why do you want to achieve these goals? Understand why they matter and why you are willing to pay a price to achieve them.

2. **Know what you are aiming at** – Set clear goals so that you know what you are working towards what you want to achieve.

3. **Break it down** – You cannot do everything at once. Attempting to do everything at once will leave you feeling overwhelmed. Focus on specific things that you want to introduce in your daily habits. Start by doing one thing consistently, and when you get that right, you can add more things.

4. **Be accountable** – Tell someone about your journey and ask them to help you stay on track. Don't be afraid to tell them if you failed or if you are struggling. They are there to support you and help to keep you on track.

5. **Review your progress and actions** – You can look back after a week and measure your progress. This will help you to identify challenges and amend your strategy. It will also help to motivate you and keep you on track. See what you have achieved in this time, know what you should change and keep an eye on your goal.

6. **Celebrate your progress** – Keep on celebrating small victories, a successful day, week, and month. Remember that the aim is to keep going - not to be flawless. Growth is your main priority.

7. **Keep yourself motivated** – Revisit your goals and vision and understand how your progress is bringing you closer to them. See the change in your habits and life and let it motivate you to keep going and keep growing.

8. **Remind and enforce** – Remind yourself why you are doing this. Know that you are not only making an impact on your life, but you are also impacting the lives of those around you.

9. **Know the enemy** – Know yourself and your weaknesses. Get a strategy to work around your weaknesses and external factors that can derail your efforts. This is an open and honest journey. You don't need to be perfect, just be accountable.

10. **Find your way back** – There is always a chance that you will fail or get derailed. This is part of the journey. Don't let it stop or break you. Find what you need to do next and continue. You will never start over because you are more experienced, smarter, and better equipped, even after failure.

11. **Be patient** – Consistency is a lifelong journey. Don't put too much pressure on yourself. You need to enjoy what you do. Try to discover something about yourself on this journey. Take it one day at a time and know that you are further than you were yesterday. Know that everything will work out for the best.

Final thought: It is important to travel through life at your own pace so that you don't lose yourself along the way.

> *Greatness comes by doing a few small and smart things each and every day. Comes from taking little steps, consistently. Comes from making a few small chips against everything in your professional and personal life that is ordinary, so that a day eventually arrives when all that's left is The Extraordinary.*
>
> **- Robin S. Sharma**

LIVE A LIFE OF IMPACT

We are on this third planet from the sun, for a very limited time. As human beings, we are created with free will. We have a choice of how we make use of our time here. What we do will eventually become someone's memory of us. The impact of our actions will be seen in the lives of others. With your life, you are creating a legacy. What that legacy will be and who it will benefit is your choice.

> *Just as ripples spread out when a single pebble is dropped into water, the actions of individuals can have far-reaching effects.*
>
> **– Dalai Lama**

We need to acknowledge that our decisions do not only impact our lives, but it also impacts the lives of those closest to us, and from there, our lives touch a much wider audience. The realization that my life is not all about me has brought me to a sudden junction, many times. It is both frightening and liberating to contemplate one's decisions and actions. The easy question is: How will it benefit me? An even better question is: How will it benefit everyone else?

Seven keys to a life of impact:

1. **Know who you are** – Be honest about who you are and where you are. In other words, discover yourself and find your journey. We need a baseline to work from, and even rock-bottom is a good baseline to start from. Use your baseline to dream about and plan your future, always keeping the impact that you want to make in this world, in mind.

2. **Care** – Everything we do, our every action affects someone. Make sure you care about the people that will be touched by your actions. If we don't care about people, then all our actions will be centred around ourselves and our own gratification in a consequence-free thought process. The moment we acknowledge that we care about people, our focus moves away from ourselves and onto the ripple effect of our actions.

3. **Be accountable** – Invite people who will keep you accountable, into your life. People that will ask the tough questions and give you an honest opinion. This "Inner Circle" is one of the keys to success. Give these people enough authority to influence you within the limits of your ethical boundaries. This also implies that you need to convince yourself that you are accountable for your decisions. Even more so, you need to convince people on the outside, that you are accountable. Keep in mind that these might be people who look at life from a different perspective and will analyse our actions much deeper than we dare to.

4. **Learn from the past** – We need to get to a point where we acknowledge the past and what it has to offer. We must learn from the action, mistakes, successes, and bravery of others. We also need to take our own history seriously and learn from our experience. We need to make our own journey and our own experience, count.

5. **Set the bar high** – We only get one chance at living this life, and we might as well throw everything at it. A good friend of mine always said that we need to live our lives to the maximum because we are a gift to this world. At the end of our lives, we should not be unopened presents, all that will be left is torn paper and a mountain of memories. Choose to live largely and impact deeply.

6. **Build your legacy** – Every person is building their own story. Everything we do is the writings in our chapters. We need to measure everything we do to the story we want people to tell about ourselves and our lives when we are not here anymore. We all have a responsibility to live our extraordinary stories.

7. **Love what you do** – If we love what we do, then we will do it with passion, purpose, courage, and inspiration. Motivation and inspiration are addictive. The love we have for what we do will rub off on people. It will impact their lives deeply, touching the core of their existence. We will inspire people because our focus is on giving and creating value by building into the lives of others. People will be inspired by our enthusiasm and by the legacy we create and the quality that we give.

Final thought: We have one shot at living an extraordinary life and we need to make it count from our first step.

> *" The greatness of a man is not in how much wealth he acquires, but in his integrity and his ability to affect those around him positively. "*
>
> **- Bob Marley**

TELL YOUR STORY

You are the author and the narrator of your own story. You have the choice of what you write into your biography, and you have a choice about the way you tell your story. It is your choice from which perspective you look at your life. The fact is; it's your story.

> *" Every human is an artist. And this is the main art that we have: the creation of our story. "*
>
> **- Don Miguel Ruiz**

The 2003 movie, Big Fish, with Ewan McGregor, is a great example of how we have a choice of the story we tell about our lives. In the movie, Edward Bloom's father (played by Albert Finney) teaches his unimaginative son (Ewan McGregor) that we all have a choice of how we tell the stories of your lives. Listening to his father's colourful stories, Edward discovers how rich and precious his story can be, he just had to reimagine his own life and tell his story differently.

The way we think about our lives and the way we tell our stories and will inevitably have an effect on the way we live your lives. If we are in search of the wonderful, the colourful, and the unique, that is exactly what we will find. The opposite is unfortunately also true. In my view, we should be living our lives as explorers, all the time in search of new experiences, and seeing life as an adventure. Finding those colours in your life will help you to write a wonderful and inspirational story.

The adventures of your life will always be a part of your journey, and you need to keep them fresh. Think about them, talk about them, tell the stories, and write them down so that you don't forget them. If you let them go and forget about them, you will not have any stories to keep you company on your journey. If you don't keep your past stories in mind, you will have no stories to inspire you while you are trying to make sense of your current chapter. A story is a wonderful way of teaching and transferring knowledge. People first remember how the story made them feel and then they are reminded of the lessons.

I started telling my story in a new way, many years ago. I love my life and the incredible journey that I am on. The way I see myself and the way I tell my story kept me going through the tough times. It didn't matter how tough times were, I instinctively knew that the next adventure was just around the corner or that this moment will turn out to be an adventure. I learned to see the difficult times as part of the adventure. You cannot have an adventure without experiencing adversity. You are not in control of an adventure. You are a character in a story. You discover new things about life, people, the world, and yourself. You grow while you live through an adventure, holding-on because you know there is a great ending to this chapter.

My story gives me hope for the future because I know I have been through much worse and I am still here. I know I am here for a purpose and the best for me is yet to come. This is my adventure, and I will not let it go.

If you are not excited about your story you have a couple of choices:
- Maybe it's time to start writing a new chapter in your story. Time to make some adjustments to your life to get your story in-line

with your vision for your life.

- Maybe it's time to start looking in a new way at your current chapter. Finding the quality, the highlights, the experience, the special, precious, and beautiful moments in your chapter.

Final thought: Make sure your life's story is a story worth telling. A story that will inspire generations to come.

> *My story is a freedom song of struggle. It is about finding one's purpose, how to overcome fear and to stand up for causes bigger than one's self.*
>
> **- Coretta Scott King**

CULTIVATE A FORWARD REACHING MINDSET

A forward reaching mindset or as I fondly refer to it: A Grappling Hook mindset, is a strategy I came up with while going through adversity. A grappling hook mindset is one of the keys to living a remarkable life, a life of victory and significance. In life we often get hit by adversity, we don't have a choice in that fact. Life remains unpredictable at best. When we experience setbacks, we tend to do one of three things:

- We either try and Cope by finding joy, meaning and value, in what we already have.
- We isolate ourselves to find our balance and stabilize the situation or just hide from reality.
- We Reach forward and grab onto something that will pull us forward and out of the situation. I often use the analogy of throwing a Grappling Hook forward and then pulling myself towards that point.

> *The will to win, the desire to succeed, the urge to reach your full potential… these are the keys that will unlock the door to personal excellence.*
>
> **- Confucius**

A forward reaching mindset starts exactly where it says, in your mind. You make a conscious decision to keep on moving forward and growing no matter what life throws at you. The advantage of a Grappling Hook mindset is that it takes us out of our current situation/challenges and moves our focus to the future and onto possibilities. This mindset keeps the dream alive by pointing us towards our potential, not our challenges.

When we go through adversity and reach for the quality items in life, items like goals, caring, giving, growing and inspiration, we need to take our focus off our current situation. This happens because, in the centre of our humanity, we believe that the best is yet to come. Because a forward-reaching mindset is future-focused, we know that this is not the end of our story, this is the making of a stronger me. This is the route we take on our journey to a remarkable life. My goals, hopes, and dreams are my grappling hooks that get me through tough times. I pull myself up, and forward, by them.

I remember one afternoon we got trapped in a snowstorm while on our way to summit Mount Kilimanjaro. In the chaos and uncertainty of that moment, I remember saying to myself "Keep moving, you are not here for this storm, you are here to summit this mountain. You are here on purpose and with a purpose."

That "Summit" Grappling Hook got me to where I needed to be. It did not take the danger away, but it helped me to focus on what was more important than the storm. It dragged me through and out of the storm by allowing me to keep my focus and making sure I maintained momentum through inspiration and sheer determination.

> *When you reach the end of your rope, tie a knot in it and hang on.*

- Franklin D. Roosevelt

Six questions to cultivate a forward-reaching mindset:
1. What do I still want to do in my lifetime?
2. What is important to me?
3. Who is important to me?
4. What stories do I want people to tell about my life?
5. What makes me truly happy?
6. What inspires me?

Final thought: Take the opportunity and grow into the person you want to be. Use your grappling hooks to get yourself moving and then take small steps to get to where you want to be.

> *Success is no accident. It is hard work, perseverance, learning, studying, sacrifice and most of all, love of what you are doing or learning to do.*

- Pele

FIND THE COURAGE TO CONTINUE

> *Success is not final; failure is not fatal: it is the courage to continue that counts.*
>
> **– Winston Churchill**

These words of Winston Churchill get so much meaning when I look at successful people. Their history not only tells stories of failure but is dominated by stories of courage, resilience, mental toughness, and agility. They have an undying will to get up. You see, it's not the people who never fail, who are successful. It is those who fail but who get up anyway to try again. Those who can take failure in their stride and almost immediately get up. Successful people are those that can turn failure into an advantage or even into an opportunity. Those are the people you should stick close to.

Failure is just another opportunity to experience life from a different perspective. Failure gives you the opportunity to learn, become wiser, adapt your strategy, and come back stronger than ever. The key is to always get up after failure, no matter what you feel or what anyone is telling you. This is your life and you have a choice of how you live it. This is your story and it matters. Don't get stuck at your last failure and live a defeated life. Get motivated by your last failure, get up, adapt your strategy, and plan, and come back stronger. Live a life of victory by being strong enough to get up and courageous enough to try again.

> *"You gain strength, courage, and confidence by every experience in which you really stop to look fear in the face. You are able to say to yourself, 'I lived through this horror. I can take the next thing that comes along.'"*
>
> **- Eleanor Roosevelt**

8 Strategies to bounce back from failure:

1. **Accept change** – Life is going to be different, accept it. There is a huge difference between "Different" and "Bad", both are available, and you must choose. Accept that you need to adapt with the times, accept that change is inevitable, and that failure is not fatal.

2. **Be honest with yourself** – To be able to learn from your mistakes and failures, you need to be honest with yourself. Honesty will assist you to get to the bottom of the reason for the failure. This helps you to understand what happened and assists you to put a strategy and mechanisms in place to prevent a recurrence. By doing this you are making your armour stronger.

3. **Build strong relationships** – with people that support, motivate, and inspire you to keep trying again. They are the people that will help you get back on your feet after setbacks.

4. **Act** – The biggest challenge you will have is to start again. Start by doing small things that bring joy and energy to your life. Think about things that excite and inspire you and then start moving towards them. Find happiness by doing the little things well.

5. **Be your own best friend** – Don't beat yourself up over what happened. Be gentle with yourself and make a list of what your values and qualities are. Be proud of the human you were created as.

6. **Make a Happy List** – Make a list of things that give you joy and bring happiness to your life. Do these things more often.

7. **Focus on others rather than on your challenges** – By giving to others we discover a part of ourselves. Giving brings joy and purpose to our lives. Giving helps us to find our value and rediscover our self-confidence.

8. **Set those goals** – Goals are the grappling hooks that we pull yourself forward by. It can get us out of the biggest slumps. Set small and big goals and start hunting them down.

Final thought: You are stronger than you think you are. Believe in yourself and in your potential. The smallest piece of inspiration can get you out of the deepest hole.

> *Hope lies in dreams, in imagination, and in the courage of those who dare to make dreams into reality.*
>
> **- Jonas Salk**

GIVE YOURSELF TIME TO HEAL

In today's society, I find that we cultivate the perception that everything, including ourselves, must be great, all the time. People seem to think that something is wrong when "something is wrong". Having a bad day, then turns into a crisis because according to us, it should not happen. While "having a bad day" is just another part of being human. We live in a broken world, on a volatile planet in an uncontrollable universe. We are not in control and that is the way it should be.

> *Some days are just bad days, that's all. You have to experience sadness to know happiness, and I remind myself that not every day is going to be a good day, that's just the way it is!*
>
> **- Dita Von Teese**

We cannot have good days if we don't know what it means to have bad days. We need the contrast of life to understand and become fully functional and in-tune, humans. So, give yourself a break and admit that today is maybe not as good as the other days. Understand that it's also okay to not be okay. There is no schedule, cycle or rule that tells us how we should feel or what emotions we are supposed to have. Don't be hard on yourself and don't try to force your way out of your current emotion. Accept it for what it is and rather find a way to bring joy, a better understanding of yourself and healing into your life.

12 Pieces of advice to help you to heal and to find joy in today:

1. Acknowledge that it is okay to have a bad day. A bad day doesn't mean that something is wrong with you.
2. Know that you don't need to explain to anyone why you feel this way.
3. Understand that this is just one of many days in your life and this is just one of many emotions in your life.
4. Recognize that you can find meaning and a better understanding, in today.
5. Tell yourself that you are valuable and we as human beings need your uniqueness. You matter.
6. Find one thing that you value and be thankful for it.
7. Think of one person that you love and be happy and thankful for that person.
8. Think of one thing that you like about yourself and then, appreciate it.
9. Think of one thing that you still want to do and be excited about it.
10. Go for a walk, smell the fresh air, and appreciate nature.
11. Have some coffee or tea.
12. Know that tomorrow will be a better day.

Final thought: We are not in control, we are travellers through time, writing our stories. Take a deep breath and relax with the understanding that you don't need to be in control. You are here to observe life and to help others to experience life.

> *Love yourself for who you are, and trust me, if you are happy from within, you are the most beautiful person and your smile is your best asset.*

- Ileana D'Cruz

FIND MEANING IN THE CONTRASTS OF LIFE

Many of us are under the impression that the natural state of life is intended to be effortless. We anticipate a life without challenges or setbacks. This could not be further from the truth. We live in an unpredictable environment in a fast-paced and ever-changing world. A world filled with uncertainty, unexpected. We are not in control of the world and neither are we in control of the actions of other people. We can actually only be in control of our attitude and the way we live our lives. So, what does life in an unpredictable world, filled with unpredictable people, mean?

> *" You should never view your challenges as a disadvantage. Instead, it's important for you to understand that your experience facing and overcoming adversity is actually one of your biggest advantages. "*
>
> **- Michelle Obama**

It means that our lives will always be filled with contrast. We first need to understand what it means to be sad before we can truly be happy. We need to experience a failure to fully appreciate success or triumph. We need to understand what suffering is before we can truly have empathy. For everything in life, there is an opposite. It is these opposites that give meaning, character, and flavour to life. It helps us to have a deeper appreciation for life and a deeper sense of what it means to be human.

The contrast of life should not only develop us on an emotional level but should also drive us to action. It is good to understand suffering and have empathy, but it is our purpose to do something about it. It is our purpose to address contrast, spending our lives in search of a better way of doing. It is our purpose to spend our lives caring for the victims of contrast.

> *Our ability to handle life's challenges is a measure of our strength of character.*
>
> **- Les Brown**

Do not see the contrast as an unnatural state of life in this world, rather see it as a natural state that gives us purpose. The natural state of things that supply us with a reason for being.

12 Ways to live in a world of contrast:
1. Set clear priorities for your life.
2. Know your values and stick to it.
3. Care for those around you without expecting too much.
4. Be uncomfortable about injustice.
5. Appreciate what you have.
6. Don't wait for tomorrow to start living, live today.
7. Make a difference in someone's life every day.
8. Celebrate life and our ability to enjoy the contrast it holds.
9. Learn from contrast do not avoid it.
10. Be passionate about what you do so that you can inspire others with your purpose.

Final thought: The existence of contrast is proof of the need for purpose. If life had no contrast, we would have no purpose.

> *When you dance, your purpose is not to get to a certain place on the floor. It's to enjoy each step along the way.*
>
> **- Wayne Dyer**

EMIGRATE YOUR MIND

Very few people can get to the heart of their challenges at first glance. One of the reasons is because we tend to project our challenges and problems onto something or someone else. This is a very safe option because we don't run the risk of discovering that there are actual things in our lives that we need to fix. Discovering that it is us that need to change. Discovering that we are the broken gear. Discovering that we are not as perfect as we thought.

An example of my thinking is: When people emigrate to another country with a different culture, they have trouble to adapt and find it difficult to fit in. Is it because of the new culture that has a problem, or is the problem the way they experience this new culture? Are they the problem?

> *Without continual growth and progress, such words as improvement, achievement, and success have no meaning.*
>
> **- Benjamin Franklin**

We tend to transpose our problems onto something else, something not so close to who we are. Something that will not expect change from us. We need something or someone that we can blame. We go through all this effort to "resolve" a problem that is much closer to home. We spend years of our lives running into these same walls because we are looking in the wrong place for the solution.

Back to my story: The people who emigrated cannot control or change the culture of their adopted country. The only thing they can change is themselves and the way they see and experience this new culture. At first, the new culture can be a threat to them, but as soon as they decide to respect this new culture and start to discover the beauty and value it holds, their world starts to change. The new culture did not change. The change came from within. They found the power of the mind and used it effectively. They changed their world by only changing themselves and the way they see their world.

Six incredible abilities imperfect humans have:
1. Change and become better, smarter, and faster.
2. Grow and expand our minds and the way we see the world.
3. Adapt to make any situation work for us, not because the situation or environment is ideal but because we are in control of the only thing we can control ourselves.
4. Be Agile and act fast on opportunities, change and threats.
5. Be Resilient and come back after enormous setbacks. Create incredible lives out of nothing.
6. Care and therefore help people see and experience the world in a different way. Help people see the beauty in the world through your eyes.

All we need is a growth mindset, a mindset where we make self-development and growth a priority. A mindset where we keep ourselves accountable for our thoughts and actions. A mindset where we accept change as a necessary part of life. A mindset where we look critically at ourselves, not to criticize but to get to the root of problems, understand it, change ourselves, adapt to the environment and grow to live quality lives.

Final thought: The way we see the world is just the story we tell ourselves about the world. Everyone tells a different story to make sense of reality. We need a mindset where we see ourselves not as complete but as a work in progress. Emigrate your mind to the place you want to be, and your body will follow.

> *" Growth is painful. Change is painful.*
> *But, nothing is as painful as staying*
> *stuck where you do not belong. "*
>
> **- N. R. Narayana Murthy**

PART 2: LIVE WITH IMPACT

FIND YOUR MOUNTAIN MAGIC

All of us are climbing a mountain, no one else is climbing or even knows about. This mountain consists of obstacles, challenges, setbacks, opportunities and potential. Your mountain is unique and unexplored. You are the first to attempt to summit it. All the time you are trying to get on to the next ridge or just get a solid foothold so that you can catch our breath. We are inching forward into the unknown.

I love climbing and climbing mountains has given me many valuable lessons. Lessons I use every day to climb my mountain of life. I call it: my Mountain Magic.

> *There's a constant tension in climbing, and really all exploration, between pushing yourself into the unknown but trying not to push too far. The best any of us can do is to tread that line carefully.*
>
> **- Alex Honnold**

I have climbed many mountains and rock faces in my life, each one unique. Each one presented me with unique challenges but also with an incredibly unique experience. Each one had a personality of their own and required me to adapt to get to the top.

10 Principles of my mountain magic:

1. **What is my purpose** – I need to know why I am climbing this mountain. I must have an answer to the question: Why? This gives me purpose, a goal, motivation and helps me to focus on what is important.

2. **Do the basics well** – When things go wrong, I make sure that I do those things that are within my control, well. I go back to basics and lay a solid foundation.

3. **Consistency is key** – A constant pace and good habits will get me there much faster than a fast pace. Consistency helps me to enjoy the climb but also keep me safe from the dangers of speed.

4. **Learn from those who went before me** – I don't try and reinvent the wheel, I rather learn from those with more experience than me. I love to learn from those who already stood at the summits of mountains.

5. **Plan your climb** – I do the hard work before I start the climb. Days, weeks and months of research and training help me to get to my goal with fewer setbacks and challenges. It makes me emotional and physically stronger and better prepared than the next person. I strive to be the person people come to for advice, but to be that person takes a lot more than just being.

6. **Make use of quality gear and people** – When we use substandard or unreliable equipment, they will fail us when we need them most. The same applies to people.

7. **Take it slow** – Climbing a mountain is not a race and neither is life. The less we rush the more we can enjoy the experience and appreciate the view. By being composed we reduce the risks we can come across.

8. **Appreciate the view from where you are** – There are no guarantees that I will reach the top so I might as well look up and enjoy the view, right there where I am. Enjoy the moment and love the climb.

9. **There is always another route** – When I get stuck, I turn back to find another route. Waiting while being stuck will not change the mountain. I need to change; I need to let go of my ego and climb down so that I can find a new route. I am the movable object in the equation.

10. **Fear is part of the journey** – A lot of times when I get to the top of a rock face my hands are shaking. Yes, I am tired. Yes, the adrenaline is pumping but the truth is that there is always fear in the equation. I need a bit of fear. Fear keeps me honest and it helps me to maintain my focus. Fear keeps me from becoming reckless. In the end, a manageable amount of fear keeps me safe.

Final thought: My philosophy about mountains is: We can never conquer mountains, we are just allowed a short time on them to view the world from a different angle and then we need to go down as changed beings, while the mountain remains the same.

> *Climb the mountain not to plant your flag, but to embrace the challenge, enjoy the air and behold the view. Climb it so you can see the world, not so the world can see you.*
>
> **- David McCullough Jr.**

BE THE ESCAPE ROUTE

We live in a broken world filled with broken people. We don't need to look far to find people who went through or are going through terrible times. People having to deal with the worst that life has to offer. People having to carry unbearable hurt while still expected to function the way society dictates. We can easily feel overwhelmed by the sheer size of emotional and physical destruction around us. Although we cannot address everyone's pain, we can make a difference in some lives. We can help people escape for a while.

A mistake I have made many times is to talk to people about their pain and their struggles. A couple of years ago, when I went through hard times, and during this period, I realized why my strategy was so ineffective. I realized that I did not want to talk about my challenges all the time. I wanted to be free of them. I wanted to think and talk about something else. I wanted to talk about things that would lift my spirit and inspire me. I found that if I talked about myself and my problems, I became the problem. I became trapped in my circumstances, and people kept me there by caring "too" much. By asking how I was doing, people were reminding me of my situation and pushing me back into the "Hole". All I wanted was to be free of the challenges I was facing and not be reminded of them.

During this time, I learned a very valuable lesson from a friend. This friend never asked me how I was doing or what was happening with my challenges. I knew I could talk to him at any time. I knew he was there for me. We drank coffee and talked about life, sports, politics, family and just about everything else. We played golf, went on hikes and took long drives. He asked for my advice. He asked me to help him with some of his challenges. Today I understand what he did, and I have so much respect for him. What did he do?

He set me free from my situation. He opened my cage. He dragged me out of "The Hole". By treating me as just another person, he made me feel normal again. He took me out of my situation and helped me to find my life and my value. By asking for my help, he showed me that I had value, and I was not "my circumstances" I was just in "circumstances" outside my control. With a soft approach, he forced me to add value to those around me and in doing so, rediscover my own value.

> **❝** *The friend in my adversity I shall always cherish most. I can better trust those who helped to relieve the gloom of my dark hours than those who are so ready to enjoy with me the sunshine of my prosperity.* **❞**
>
> ### - Ulysses S. Grant

We set people free by talking to them about "something else". Talk about all the things we usually talk about, things that make us laugh, cry, and angry. Talk about things that excite, inspire and the things that give us hope.

By treating people this way, you open the door for them to feel "normal" again. They start to feel like they are part of society and has a role to play. You make them feel needed. With conversation we set people free, bring back "normal", we bring hope and inspiration. Because we are social beings, conversation brings life.

What can we do for people going through tough times? Start by doing the following:

1. **Be available** – Make sure they know that you are there for them. Make an effort to stay in contact.

2. **Listen** – Let them talk. Give them an opportunity to talk about anything even if they keep on repeating their current story.

3. **Talk** – Talk to them about "something else". Widen the discussion and explore new topics. Challenge people to think about new things or think in different ways about old things.

4. **Remind them** – They are still valuable, and they just need to be reminded of that fact, now and then.

5. **Act** – Take them outside and do things with them. Have fun and show them that there is life out there.

6. **Future** – Help them to find their dreams and goals again. Help them to start believing in the future, again.

7. **Ask** – Ask for advice and help. It will make them feel valuable if they can add value to your life. They will find purpose.

Final thought: We set people free by taking them out of their circumstances and showing them a world outside the fog that is clouding their reality.

> *" Be strong, be fearless, be beautiful. And believe that anything is possible when you have the right people there to support you. "*
>
> **- Misty Copeland**

ROLL WITH THE PUNCHES OF LIFE

On a cool evening in March 1966, in Toronto, Canada, little known, hard-hitting Canadian boxer, George Chuvalo showed the world another side of losing. On March 26, 1966, the invincible Muhammad Ali flew over the Canadian border for a "formality", just another bout before he could face the "real" contenders. Little had he known that March 26 would be the fight of his life. Although Ali lost fights later on in his career, he was in the form of his life when he flew over the border. Chuvalo was tough, smart and prepared to pay the price. He knew what it would take to bring Ali, down. That night George Chuvalo took everything Ali could throw at him. He knew exactly what was coming and he was willing to pay the price. Amid Ali's onslaught, Chuvalo took every punch and kept on moving forward. Chuvalo knew Ali would be exhausted by round 15 and this would give him the opportunity he was looking for. It happened exactly like he planned, by round 15 Ali was so exhausted he could barely stand up. Through a combination of determination and sheer luck, Ali remained standing and survived when the bell rang for the end of the match. Ali won on points but Chuvalo won the fight. Afterwards, Ali was rushed to hospital with a bleeding kidney and spent the night in the hospital while George Chuvalo took a shower and then took his wife dancing.

George Chuvalo knew how to take punches, how to absorb punches and how to roll with the punches. He was not avoiding them, he was expecting them. He knew what to do with a punch and how to keep his focus on his goal. After March 26, Chuvalo became known as the "Toughest man in boxing".

In the years that followed, George Chuvalo lost his three sons and his wife to addiction, suicide and overdose. Chuvalo was tougher outside the ring than inside. He used every ounce of his strength to survive a life that sounds more like a tale of tragedy.

> *The deaths of the four people closest to him were staggering blows — the toughest man in boxing was overwhelmed. Bedridden by the sheer cruelty of fate. But Chuvalo drew on endless reserves of perseverance and has emerged as an eloquent anti-drug advocate and public speaker.*
>
> **- David Giddens**

11 Lessons I learned from George Chuvalo:

1. Don't expect anything to be easy.
2. Train harder than anyone else.
3. Expected the hard blows whether you see them coming or not.
4. Have a strategy to deal with the blows of life.
5. There is no place for ego in a purpose-driven life.
6. Know what you value and fight for it.
7. If life knocks you down, come back stronger. Someone is always watching.
8. Know the price you are willing to pay.
9. Value those you love; they will not always be there.
10. In life, you can lose the game and still win the fight.
11. Don't let the punches break you, let them make you.

Final thought: I have the greatest respect for George Chuvalo because he was not a saint, he was a fighter that came from nowhere and excelled. He is a human with real battles and real solutions. He made mistakes, admitted them and changed his ways. He took everything life could throw at him and still made an enormous positive impact on the world around him. His story is not a fairy tale but a tale of guts, perseverance and sheer determination.

> *Face your problems head-on. Do what you have to do to take care of it. Develop a good work ethic.*
>
> **- George Chuvalo**

BECOME A FACILITATOR FOR SUCCESS

In these exciting times, leaders and leadership are the topics in many a conversation. We can talk as much as we like about leadership but if there are no followers, no support, no execution of vision then there is no leadership. Society needs more quality leaders, but also has a desperate requirement for people who understand the meaning of followers, supporters, and executioners of vision. I am not referring to passive followers, but I am talking about empowered people who understand the vision, buy into it and can execute it.

I am saying this because it is our responsibility to ensure that our leaders are ethical, set quality goals, remain on track, and become successful. We are the ones who empower our leaders, who make them strong and who can help them become successful. Whether we talk about leaders in sports, religion, organisations, or even political leaders, we must take responsibility to ensure that they remain on track and execute their mandate ethically and effectively. We should walk away from the victim mentality and get ourselves into an empowered and accountability mindset. We cannot change the past, but we can actively shape the future.

> **❝** *Choose to focus your time, energy and conversation around people who inspire you, support you and help you to grow you into your happiest, strongest, wisest self.* **❞**
>
> **- Karen Salmansohn**

We must play an active supporting role in leadership to be part of the solution. It is our responsibility to develop and grow our leaders into success.

> *Irrespective of any political party, I am a supporter of good people who want to do something for society.*
>
> **- Kapil Dev**

10 Steps to become a facilitator for success:

1. **Focus on success** – Our focus should be on making our leaders successful. If our leaders are successful it means that we are also part of their success and will benefit from the rewards of their success.

2. **Have a collective approach** – Involve everyone necessary to make the leader successful. We don't need to do everything on your own. Get help, involve, delegate, and associate.

3. **Become a success generator** – Don't just aim to make one person successful. Aim to make everyone you can, successful. Let the habit become a mindset. Find unique solutions for unique situations and unique people.

4. **Be actively available** – Be actively involved and available to the leaders you are assisting. Don't wait for them to call on you. Take responsibility for them and make sure you stay on top of whatever is happening to and around them. Stay in constant contact with them. Care enough to be there for them.

5. **Communicate effectively** – Success and communication go hand in hand. We need to be able to communicate effectively in the environment we are operating in. This means we must be excellent listeners, great interpreters, and excellent speakers. Translate and relay communication from different sources to your leaders. Help them to make quality decisions based on quality understanding, insight, and interpretations. Take the emotion out of communication and find the essence of the message.

6. **Keep an eye on the horizon** – We need to understand the world you are operating in. We need to be able to identify potential problems, threats, and issues early to inform our leadership timeously of what is on the way. We are our leaders second set of senses.

7. **Be a source of energy and Motivation** – People get tired and run out of energy. It is our responsibility to be the energy to our leaders. To pick them up when they are down, to motivate them and get them back on track.

8. **Become a mainstay** – Leaders are under immense pressure, coming from all directions. We should ask ourselves how we can alleviate some of that pressure. How can we lighten the load by taking some of the responsibility onto ourselves? Be active in the pursuit to resolve issues that result in pressure and stress. You view the situation from a different and unique perspective. Use your insight to alleviate pressure and create success.

9. **Think process** – Leaders are strategic thinkers. They know where they want to head and why they want to go there. They sometimes lack the process to get there. Help them to identify the steps and actions that need to be taken to reach the common goal.

10. **Develop your emotional awareness** – Be sensitive to a leader's emotional state. Get to know them so that you will be able to see when they are going through challenging times and need additional emotional support.

Final thought: A great portion of the potential for success, of the people around us, resides within our grasp. In playing an active role in guiding people to become successful, we become facilitators for success.

> *Be strong, be fearless, be beautiful. And believe that anything is possible when you have the right people there to support you.*
>
> **- Misty Copeland**

THE KEYS TO A REMARKABLE LIFE

PART 3:

HAVE A MIRACLE MINDSET

FIND YOUR RECIPE TO BOUNCE BACK AFTER ADVERSITY

Every person has a unique recipe that helps us get up and come back from adversity. The recipe is made up of various ingredients and the aim of the recipe is not to solve your problems or take away your challenges. The recipe is there to help you get the gears of your life moving again.

Sometimes we are so stuck that we just don't know what to do, where to go or even what to think. By using your recipe, you can get the gears in your life moving again. This will help you to get moving, gain momentum and even find some inspiration.

Ask yourself: If I do not use my recipe and get up, where will this leave me? If not for today, think about your future and the future of the lives of the people, you touch. You are not done yet, you are just stuck. Call it a bad place or call it what you want, the fact is that you are here now, and you need to move on because there is a life ahead of you. Your action doesn't need to be pretty or graceful - just get yourself up and moving. Momentum will do the rest. You have more power, resilience, motivation, and inspiration in you than you ever knew. Get up and do the basics really well. Before you know it, you would be the inspirational one that everybody is talking about.

I need the following ingredients to get myself up and start moving. I do not just use them once; I use them daily and some I use even more frequent. When you go through adversity, you will need to make the task of picking yourself up a priority until it becomes a habit. Doing it once will not be enough; it is not a miracle potion. It is a recipe that you can use to build an extraordinary comeback and that will give you an amazing testimony if you stick with it. Your recipe will look different from mine, but then again, we will probably share some of the same ingredients to create something really special.

Six ingredients of my recipe to bounce back:

1. **Goals** – Give direction and purpose. It gives me something to aim at and to work towards.

2. **Meditation** – This is a time to get in touch with yourself. Personal time is where you can be honest about where you are so that you can understand what you need to do to get where you are going.

3. **An early start** – Get up early and make sure the day does not get away from you. I want to be up before the activity starts. I want to feel part of the awakening of the day. This gives me the impression that I have an active role to play in this day.

4. **Exercise** – Generates energy and energy stimulates inspiration. When I exercise, I revisit my goals to keep them fresh in my mind. I make sure that I am on top of whatever I am chasing. In these moments of free-thinking, I discover a new insight, come up with new ideas and sometimes I even revise my strategy to be more relevant towards my goals.

5. **Hydrate** – Studies have shown that several ailments are a result of dehydration. A lack of concentration and the inability to remember can at times also be attributed to dehydration.

6. **Breath** – One small thing that really works well is to focus on your breathing. We tend to move into a cycle of shallow breathing when we are under stress, depriving our bodies of enough oxygen to operate at optimal levels. Without enough oxygen we

cannot think clearly, our muscles cannot operate at their best. We become a fraction of what we can be.

Final thought: You have a unique recipe that will help you bounce back from adversity. It is your responsibility to make time to discover your recipe. No one else can do it for you.

> *Today I will do what others won't, so tomorrow I can accomplish what others can't.*

- Jerry Rice

VALUE YOUR TIME

Only when we don't have time do we realize the value of time. Time is a commodity to which each person attaches his/her own value. Unfortunately, time is the one thing that cannot be bought, bargained with, or borrowed. Time either gives or it takes, the decision is yours.

> *Time is your best companion or your worst enemy. You decide.*
>
> **– Lourens Botha**

To value time, one must first admit that time is valuable. But what makes time so valuable? You need to figure that out for yourself.

I found the value of time because time gave me the opportunity to:

- be with the people I love.
- discover me, my purpose, and my passion.
- develop myself to be able to live the life I wanted.
- chase my dreams and goals.
- experience the thrill of victory and the pain of defeat.
- laugh and love without measure.
- get hurt, to cry and to heal.
- be scared, although I choose not to remain there for too long.
- be brave and overcome what I feared.
- be angry at injustice but also to do something about it.
- discover happiness and love.

- feel the pain of others.
- appreciate my senses.
- see people get up from the worst setbacks and circumstances.
- fail, learn, grow and to get back up. To coming back stronger.
- be inspired.
- travel the world and appreciate the diversity of humanity.
- seek spirituality and gain an understanding of my place in the universe.
- be unique.
- experience how fragile and precious life is.

We must accept that we cannot control time, we can only manage it. We will either manage our time or time will manage us. In the end, time will keep on ticking by, no matter what we do, so make sure you use the time you have.

Seven strategies to manage time:

1. **Value time** – If you do not value your time you will also not value the time of others. This mindset can cost you more than just time, in the end.

2. **Goals** – An effective way to help you to focus on a result is to have goals. Goals compel you to focus a specific result and in so doing keep you moving forward and on-track.

3. **Plan** – A plan is your guide to what must happen next. A plan takes the speculation out of the next step. It gives us a foundation to build on.

4. **Stress** – Stress will never give you additional time. Stress does only one thing with your precious time, it takes it away. When you stress, revisit your goal and your plan, rather spend your time there.

5. **Act** – Without action, you will be a spectator of time rushing you by.

6. **Priorities** – Make sure you do what is necessary, what is right and what is urgent, in the right sequence.

7. **Accountability** – Always have travel companions, these people can help you to use your time effectively and efficiently. These are the people who ask the tough questions and keep you accountable.

Final thought: Time gives, but it is in our hands how much and what we allow time to give.

> *Learn to enjoy every minute of your life. Be happy now. Don't wait for something outside of yourself to make you happy in the future. Think how precious is the time you have to spend, whether it's at work or with your family. Every minute should be enjoyed and savoured.*
>
> **- Earl Nightingale**

LEAD BY EXAMPLE

The reason why I do not like giving once-off motivational talks is that I discovered a long time ago that out of an audience of a thousand people there is maybe one person that can take the motivation, direction, and ideas and turn his/her life around. In other words, very few people can make a course correction without constant external intervention and support.

> *All you need is the plan, the road map, and the courage to press on to your destination.*
>
> **- Earl Nightingale**

I don't like to be called a motivational speaker because I believe motivation is just a by-product, a result that occurs when people are focused on doing what they love, doing what they are good at, are inspired by where they are heading and have the resolve to get there. Motivation is not a song played before the "Big Game" or an energetic talk by a highly motivated speaker. That type of motivation will last you just as long as your ride home. If you are part of the other 999 people in the audience, you will need help to change course, help to turn your hopes into dreams, your dreams into goals, and your goals into action. We need help to get there, we need help to achieve what we think will just remain an adrenaline-fuelled thought deep inside us.

> *The only person you are destined to become is the person you decide to be.*
>
> **- Ralph Waldo Emerson**

People will grow and change when you care enough to show up and journey with them. The most beautiful words, lines, phrases, and quotes will not get people to where they need to go. They need you to believe in them and, to be with them every step of the way. They need to be picked up, guided, inspired, and kept accountable. Success is the journey of people who pitch up, every day, and who do not take "No" for an answer. Don't be a voice in the passing, be a companion on the journey.

> **"** *Change is one of the most unexplored journeys and an underrated adventure.* **"**
>
> **– Lourens Botha**

9 Ways to lead by example:

1. **Take responsibility** – You need to set an example with the way you live your life. If your life and your story are inspirational, then people will follow your example and believe that the impossible is possible.

2. **Be accountable** – Don't be afraid to show that you are human, that you have emotions, and that you also sometimes fail. People will respect you for that, and if they don't, it's better to part ways. If the people you lead think you never fail or make mistakes, they will give up the first time they fail because your standards will be too high for them.

3. **Be courageous** – Leading with courage implies that you need to go where most fear to go. You need to take risks and do the things most people will not even attempt. You need to live life outside your Comfort Zone, all the time en route. Your goal is

always your next destination. The key here is: You need to know where you are going and why you are going there.

4. **Cultivate a growth mindset** – Make it a priority to keep on investing in yourself and others. Keep on learning and growing to become a better version of yourself. Invest in your development so that you can maximize your impact on the lives of others.

5. **Listen** – You first need to understand the person and know where they want to go before you can help them get there. Help people to get where they need to be, not where you want them to be.

6. **Trust** – This journey is about mutual trust. When we trust from both sides, there will be enough breathing room for everyone to be themselves and do what they need to do. You cannot force people into lasting change. You are a guide, not a dictator.

7. **Take care of yourself** – It takes a couple of seconds for people to form an opinion of you. That first impression will last a long time and will be extremely difficult to change. Take care of yourself by taking responsibility for your physical, emotional, and spiritual growth. People will first look at you and then based on their impressions of you, decide whether they are going to follow your example or not.

8. **Be the example** – People will listen to your words, but they will learn from your example. Inspire people by what you do, not by what you say.

9. **Show up** – People don't need your big words, your impressive title, or your long list of academic achievements. They need you! They need you to care, they need you to show up, and they need you to be there. They need you to pick them up, they need you

to advise and support them, they need you to inspire them, and they need you to succeed with them. If you take the "you" out of this equation then all people are left with is "they need", they are on their own and need to fend for themselves.

Final thought: The secret to living by example is to enjoy what you do, to know where you are going, and to know why you want to be there.

> " *The reality is that the only way change comes is when you lead by example.* "
>
> **- Anne Wojcicki**

WIN THE BATTLE BETWEEN COMFORT AND WILLPOWER

Have you ever tried to start exercising after gaining some weight or becoming unfit? Not that easy, is it? One of the hardest things we can do is to get ourselves moving. It is even harder to get ourselves moving in a new direction, doing something different or new. We are creatures of habit and comfort, and for that reason, we don't easily move, especially not when it's in a new direction. By breaking a habit, you are forcing yourself out of your comfort zone, you are forcing yourself into a new way of thinking and a new way of doing. The question is: what will win, your comfort zone or your willpower?

> *In the absence of willpower, the most complete collection of virtues and talents is wholly worthless.*
>
> **- Aleister Crowley**

10 Steps to help your willpower overcome your comfort:

1. **Set your goals** – If you want to go anywhere you need to know where you are going, first. Setting goals gives us direction and a target to aim at. It keeps us focused and helps us to keep moving when times are tough.

2. **Make a plan** – A goal without a plan will remain a dream. Make sure you understand what needs to be done to achieve your goals. Write the steps down so that you have a plan to refer to and don't get lost in the effort.

3. **Know your "Why"** – Whether you are chasing a big goal or just completing a daily task, if you do not know why you are doing it, you will lose interest fast and stop doing it. Make sure you set goals that you want to achieve, not goals that will impress people.

4. **Understand your weaknesses** – If we understand our weaknesses and our blind spots, we can get help and people to keep us accountable and make sure that we do not stumble at the first hurdle.

5. **Double-check your decisions** – Weigh all your choices with your goals. Make sure that whatever you decide will bring you closer to your goals and the life you want.

6. **Remove temptation** – If you know yourself and your weaknesses, you will also know what will tempt you to stop chasing your goals. Remove those items, people, and thoughts. Get quality people to keep you accountable and on track.

7. **Build habits** – Understand that you will only achieve your goals if you do the small things required, daily. Build those quality habits and routines into your daily schedule so that it becomes part of your life.

8. **Believe in yourself** – If you don't believe that you can achieve something, you will not achieve it. Believe in your unlimited potential and your ability to adapt, grow and be successful.

9. **Celebrate small victories** – Be proud of your effort and celebrate every step of the way. Know that you are on your way, and each day is filled with victories.

10. **Learn from failure and setbacks** – Don't be stopped by setbacks. Learn from them but keep your eyes on your goal. If you need to start over, then start over. Your goal remains the same, still

> waiting for you to arrive. Accept the fact that you took a step back but know that you are now wiser and more determined.

Final thought: Life will always be a battle between Comfort and Willpower. The one you feed the most will eventually destroy the other. Which one are you feeding?

> *" The achievements of willpower are almost beyond computation. Scarcely anything seems impossible to the man who can will strongly enough and long enough. "*
>
> **- Orison Swett Marden**

DISCOVER YOUR POTENTIAL

Many times, I have seen people question their ability rather than acknowledging their potential. When they get to the challenging times of life, they don't see adversity as an obstacle that can be overcome, they see adversity as a result of their imperfection and lack of ability. This mindset multiplies any challenge that comes across our journey. Suddenly the smallest challenge becomes a mountain because we only see inability and no potential.

> *Believe in yourself, and the rest will fall into place. Have faith in your own abilities, work hard, and there is nothing you cannot accomplish.*
>
> **- Brad Henry**

The moment we focus on our extraordinary ability to overcome adversity and our unlimited potential, our problems, challenges and adversity start to diminish. The problem literally gets cut down to size. We begin to see adversity as a part of life through which we can gain experience, learn, and grow. We acknowledge adversity as that part of life which makes us smarter and stronger. That part of life that equips us to play a "hands-on" role in, not only our lives but the lives of others.

The most successful people are not those who never made mistakes or those who do not have challenges. They are probably also not the people who came up with the best solutions or the most brilliant ideas. The most successful people are those people who never gave up even when they did not know what to do next. This is because they have confidence in their ability. Even if they do not have the answer or see a way out, they keep their focus on the big picture of their lives. They know where they came from, where they are and where they are headed. They know the route they want to travel, and they keep their focus on the result they are aiming at. They view everything between this moment and the moment they achieve their next goal, as obstacles that they will overcome.

10 tips for success from Richard Branson:

1. **Follow your dreams** – You will live a much better life if you just do it and pursue your passions. Those people who spend their time working on things they love are usually the ones enjoying life the most. They are also the ones who dared to take a risk and chase their dreams.

2. **Do some good** – If you aren't making a positive difference to other people's lives, then you shouldn't be in business. Companies have a responsibility to make a difference in the world, for their staff, their customers – everyone.

3. **Believe in your ideas** – Belief in yourself and belief in your ideas can make all the difference between success and failure. If you aren't proud of your idea and don't believe in your plans, why should anybody else?

4. **Have fun** – Fun is one of the most important - and underrated - ingredients in any successful venture. If you're not having fun, then it's probably time to try something else.

5. **Don't give up** – On every adventure I have been on – whether setting up a business, flying around the world in a balloon or racing across the ocean in a boat – there have been moments

when the easy thing to do would be to give up. By simply not giving up, brush yourself down and trying again, you'll be amazed by what you can achieve.

6. **Keep setting yourself new challenges** – If you don't write down your ideas, they could be gone by the morning. Write down lists to keep track of your goals, and you'll be amazed by what challenges you overcome.

7. **Learn to delegate** – The art of delegation is one of the key skills any entrepreneur can master. If you find people who can take on tasks you aren't good at, it frees you up to plan for the future. It also gives you time to spend with your family and friends, which is the most important thing of all.

8. **Look after your team** – If your staff are having fun and genuinely care about other people, they will enjoy their work more and do a better job. Find people who look for the best in others, praise rather than criticize, and love what they do.

9. **Get out there and do things** – Rather than sitting in front of a screen all your life, switch off the TV or the computer and go out into the world. There are so many fascinating people to meet, exciting adventures to embark upon and rewarding challenges to take on that there's no time to lose.

10. **When people say bad things about you, just prove them wrong** – Some people will react to success by trying to hang onto your coattails. The best thing you can do is to not only ignore them but to prove them wrong in every single way.

Final thought: Successful people are those people who keep themselves together when things are falling apart.

> *My attitude has always been if you fall flat on your face, at least you're moving forward. All you have to do is get back up and try again.*

- Richard Branson

CHASE YOUR GOALS

Goals are not only the building blocks of the life we want, but they are also the compass that steers us to the legacy we want to leave behind. Goals are the gears that get our dreams moving. Goals give purpose, direction, intention, and movement to our potential. Goals are the kinetic energy of our souls.

> *" What you get by achieving your goals is not as important as what you become by achieving your goals. "*
>
> **- Zig Ziglar**

In his book; Think and Grow Rich, Napoleon Hill talks about 6 steps to setting goals. Although Hill is talking about achieving financial goals, the principles are solid and can be used almost everywhere. I found it valuable in my life and in my practice. His advice forms the basis when I set goals in my own life but also when I coach teams and individuals and help them to set and achieve goals.

Six steps of goal setting by Napoleon Hill:

1. **Your goal must be specific** – You must be able to measure it. It should almost be tangible. Living a great life, for instance, is not a goal. It is a philosophy. Winning a race, climbing a mountain, receiving a qualification or getting a position in an organization, all qualify as goals. Losing weight is not a goal but losing 10 kilograms is a goal. Think about the goals and philosophy you have in your life. Your philosophy will guide you when setting

your goals. If your philosophies are strong and ethical, then your goals will be the same.

2. **Write down your goals** – To think or dream of achieving a goal motivates us but writing our goals down and being able to see it, commits us to the goal. A friend of mine always talks about the link between your hand and your brain. Putting our goal on paper activates it in our brains. We are in fact, pulling the trigger on our goals. It's a contract with yourself.

3. **Develop a plan to achieve your goals** – Break a goal down into portions with deadlines. That way things don't become too big, too much or just too fuzzy. We are able to keep more accurate track of our progress and it gives us the opportunity to celebrate each milestone we reach. Celebrating milestone keeps us motivated because it shows that we are moving forward and making progress.

4. **You must have a specific time-frame** – A goal without a time-frame is just a dream. A time-frame keeps me accountable for action and progress. If you fall behind, you need to work harder to catch-up or re-evaluate your strategy.

5. **What price am I willing to pay?** – This principle not only refers to a financial commitment but also to energy, time, luxuries, your comfort zone and many more. In John C. Maxwell's, The 21 Irrefutable Laws of Leadership, he speaks about The law of sacrifice. The law states "A Leader must give up to go up". Even our leadership ability is linked to sacrifice. The single most important question I can ask myself an almost any situation is: What price am I willing to pay?

6. **Think about your goals, daily** – You have written them down, planned, scheduled and started to execute. Now you must remind yourself every day, what you want to achieve, what you must do to achieve it and what is on the schedule for today. You are on a journey and you must know exactly where you are so that you don't get lost or get off track.

Final thought: If your goals do not move your feet, motivate your heart, drive your growth, inspire you to make the world a better place, then you are setting yourself up for failure. Let your goals be the magic that opens a brand-new world.

> *If you want to be happy, set a goal that commands your thoughts, liberates your energy and inspires your hopes.*
>
> **- Andrew Carnegie**

THE ART OF LETTING GO

We are constantly bombarded with advice, self-help books, blogs, articles, discussions and many more. All telling us what to bring into your lives, what to change and what we are doing wrong. There are loads of valuable information out there, but you will only be able to absorb and reproduce a small portion of it. We are unique and each one of us needs a unique combination of factors in our lives to be able to function effectively and successfully. If we let everything into our lives, we will soon run out of emotional space. We will be filled with everything and yet, we will be empty. We will get lost in the information.

The Chinese have a saying about simplicity that goes something like this: "Empty your cup", meaning that you cannot pour into a full cup. You need to empty your cup before you start to add something new. The flip side is that if we try to fill an already full cup with something valuable it will just spill over or get so diluted that it will disappear. If we want to learn and if we want to change, we need to make space. We need to empty our cups.

> *Truth is ever to be found in simplicity, and not in the multiplicity and confusion of things.*
>
> **- Isaac Newton**

We need to learn The Art of Letting Go. The art to let go of those things that fill our lives but adds no value. Those things that are just taking up space and preventing something of value to enter your life. If you want to live a full life, you first need to find a simple life.

You first need to make space. Start by thinking about the effect the following has on your life:

1. **Objects** – What hold do material objects have on your life? Are you trying to hang onto, pay or buy something you do not need? Is the stress of this "holding on" preventing you from doing something of value, spending time with someone of value or making valuable changes to your life?

2. **Luxuries** – We all love luxuries. To be honest, for me it is wrist watches. Tag Heuer, Breitling, Omega, it doesn't matter, I love them all. Do I buy them? No, because if I do buy one, I will have to sacrifice something else of value. The financial and stress payment will eat into the quality I have in my life and will prevent me from growing or adding value to myself or others. For now, I will just glance through the store window and be happy to let them go. What luxuries do you need to leave right where they are?

3. **Expectations** – There are two types of expectations that can fill our cups and clutter our lives:

    - The expectations that we had for our lives and that did not materialize. We need to let go of the lives we did not get, the lives that we are not living. We must find ourselves at this moment and in THIS life. We can only start building from today, not from yesterday.

    - The expectations that other people had for our lives. If you keep on blaming yourself for not reaching someone else's expectations for your life you will not be able to grow and live the life you were meant to live. Set yourself free of those expectations and surprise people by living a unique and wonderful life. A life filled with love, joy, peace and gratitude.

4. **Past Mistakes** – Are you getting stuck behind mistakes you made in the past? Is your life filled with guilt and regret? If so, then there is a better way. Learn from your mistakes, change your behaviour, become smarter and show your worth by building something precious. Accept those mistakes as part of your journey, you got the experience, might as well use it. Before you don't set yourself free from those mistakes you will not be able to live a full life. Don't ignore your mistakes, acknowledge them with respect and then move on.

5. **Other people's dreams** – Are your dreams and goals your own or are they someone else's? Do you want to do something because someone else did it and it sounds great? Do you want to do it because you are envious? Chasing someone else's dreams will most likely set you up for failure or leave you feeling empty when you achieve them. Your hopes, dreams and goals are unique to your soul. They are the music of your being. You will not be fulfilled if you don't play your authentic brand of music. Find dreams and goals that speak to your soul and let the other go.

6. **Relationships** – Is your focus on those people who want to see you succeed or are you clinging to those who would love to see you, fail? If you are not in a position to cut toxic people from your life, at least move your focus to those who add value to you. Spend more time with your heart-and-energy people and less time with the toxic ones.

Final thought: Start by doing a "clutter audit" of your life. Get rid of the clutter and give yourself some breathing space. Only then can you truly find purpose, joy and peace.

> *Simple can be harder than complex: You have to work hard to get your thinking clean to make it simple. But it's worth it in the end because once you get there, you can move mountains.*
>
> **– Steve Jobs**

ENRICH YOUR LIFE WITH GREAT PEOPLE

We all have our limitations and our limitations have a direct influence on our growth and our success. If we deny our weak points and our blind spots, we will get stuck behind them, always wondering why we don't succeed. There are loads of information out there on how to be successful. Some of these are actually relevant and the rest is not. The reason is that we are fed generic recipes for growth and success. These recipes don't take your individuality into account.

These generic recipes overlook three important factors:

- Your definition of success
- Your limitations
- Your history

It does not matter how we slice it; we first need to understand ourselves before we can move forward successfully. The good news is that there are a couple of things we can put into place that will help us get where we want to go. One of the most important factors that we can use in our favour is our interaction with people. People are success accelerators. The right people can get us past a lot of obstacles including our own inadequacies, by looking out for our blind spots. The right people can also create opportunities that we aren't able to create.

> *If you want to go fast, go alone.*
> *If you want to go far, go together.*
>
> **- African Proverb**

In order to enrich our lives, we need to put ourselves in contact with new and interesting people. People that can show us different ways of thinking and doing. How to put ourselves in contact with the right people. How do we build a life-changing network?

7 Strategies for making contact with interesting people:

1. **Put yourself on the calendar** – Make use of newspapers, magazines, business and community forums, as well as your existing network of people to identify upcoming events in your area. These events will give you the opportunity to meet new influencers. Show up, introduce yourself, talk to people.

2. **Be interested in people** – Ask people what they do and what their secrets to success are. Give people the opportunity to tell their stories and share their experience and vision. Two things can happen:
   - You can either identify a need and help them address it, or
   - You can learn something and add value to your life.

3. **Stay in contact** – Building relationships implies that we need to be in contact with people on a regular basis. We cannot build relationships with people without engagement.

4. **List your questions** – A while ago I had the opportunity to listen to a talk by a world-renowned sports psychologist. I always prepare a list of questions for every engagement I attend even if I am not the speaker or the interviewer. He started the session by asking a question "Please ask me any question", the audience was caught off-guard, but not me. I looked at the top of my list and fired my first question. He walked up to me and spend the next half an hour just talking to me. I got to interview one of the best! Make your list.

5. **Listen** – When you meet new people, give them the opportunity to speak and to tell you about them.

6. **Know your audience** – Knowing what type of person you want to meet helps you identify a forum to meet them.

7. **Social Media** – Social media is a great place to make contact with new and interesting people.

Final thought: Don't forget that you are also interesting and that you bring your own unique flavour to this world.

> *" One of the most powerful networking practices is to provide immediate value to a new connection. This means the moment you identify a way to help someone, take action. "*
>
> **- Lewis Howes**

FIND A DEEPER AWARENESS FOR YOUR WORLD

In an age where information is readily available, we are constantly bombarded with opinions and questionable insights. Bombarded to the point where we filter out most of what we receive. While your information-filters are in good shape you can make this work to your advantage. If your filter let through the right level of applicable information, you can discover your truth. A problem arises when we let in "over-interpreted" information accept it as doctrine. Information that has been regurgitated enough times to give it a different look and feel. Less interpreted information gives you the freedom to discover for yourselves, make up your mind. How do you find this type of information? You discover it by being aware.

Awareness is defined as : the knowledge that something exists or understanding of a solution or subject at present based on information or experience.

> *Every human has four endowments – self-awareness, conscience, independent will and creative imagination. These give us the ultimate human freedom... The power to choose, to respond, to change.*
>
> **- Stephen Covey**

Awareness requires self-discipline, less ego, and more focus. You need to know what is important to you, your journey and your world. The "world" that you want to have an impact on, the world you want to make a difference, in. You also need to define the impact you want to make in this world. You need to define the legacy we want to leave. It is your responsibility to discover the truth for yourself rather than adopting the opinion of others. Lazy thinkers love to convert opinions into fact and doctrine. Lazy thinkers choose to judge above understanding and solving.

> *" The ultimate value of life depends upon awareness and the power of contemplation rather than upon mere survival. "*
>
> **- Aristotle**

10 Action items to increase awareness:

1. **Information** – Become inquisitive. Ask more questions and dig deeper to get to the essence. It requires action and effort to get to the essence.

2. **The result** – Let the result you are looking for, always be understanding and solving. Move away from a judgement mindset.

3. **Conversations** – You need to have face to face interaction with people. Rather than turning to Google, pick up the phone, make an appointment – chat to someone in person to get first-hand knowledge, input, etc.

4. **Fewer media** – The media (including Social Media) feeds us with an already tainted opinion. Use their subject and let their opinion go. Get to your understanding.

5. **Move** – It is essential to be for us to be part of this world if it is our vision to be part of the solution. You need to live in and discover

the world around you if you want to make an impact. You cannot isolate ourselves and still be part of the solution. Your feet must be grounded, and you need to be in contact with people.

6. **Predict** – Predicting the outcome of events it forces you to think about events. It compels you to get to a better understanding to make a more accurate prediction. By predicting the outcome, you keep the subject constantly on our radar because you are interested in the development and how it unfolds.

7. **Follow events** – You need to follow life-changing events closely. Just taking note is not enough because the result will have a direct impact on you and on your world. One glance at history does not give us the full picture or the stories behind the story.

8. **Get a different perspective** – The painting of the world gets colour when you listen to others. You get enlightened by the insight of quality people. People get released from the prison of their limited insight and understanding. They get enlightened by diversity.

9. **Care** – Only if you care will you dedicate our time and energy to understand. If you do not care, you most likely will accept the first opinion that comes along.

10. **Intention** – If your intention is to make the world a better place then you will place a high premium on what is happening and how the world is unfolding around you. You will be intent on making a difference because you understand because you gained insight. You will be aware of events because you care about the process and the result.

Final thought: Being aware helps us to stay relevant in a fast-paced and changing world. We need to understand the world in a new way if we want others to see the world in a new way.

> *Let us not look back in anger, nor forward in fear, but around in awareness.*
>
> **- James Thurber**

PART 4:

WRITE AN EXTRAORDINARY STORY

THE KEYS TO A REMARKABLE LIFE

CULTIVATE YOUR OWN HAPPINESS

I regularly come across people who are unhappy with their lives. People who actually live "normal" lives and who on the surface, seems to be happy. At first glance, there are no threatening challenges in their lives, no recent setbacks and no recent history of adversity, that can hold them back. So, what is the problem then?

> *" Learning to love yourself is like learning to walk —essential, life-changing, and the only way to stand tall. "*
>
> **- Vironika Tugaleva**

At some point, certain people start to care more for the people around them than they care for themselves. This sounds admirable until we dig a little deeper. Just as you cannot sail a ship without wind, you cannot navigate and sail through life without the wind that keeps you moving. What is this "wind" I am referring to? This wind refers to passion, joy, motivation, inspiration, acknowledgement, and accomplishment.

Sailing your life without wind will be okay at first, but soon this wind will subside. You will find yourself at a place where feelings of dissatisfaction and regret will overwhelm you. You will lose your energy, drive, and inspiration, all because you attempted to sail a ship without wind.

> *"Allow yourself to enjoy each happy moment in your life."*
>
> **– Steve Maraboli**

10 Strategies to get the wind back into your sails:

1. Plan the holiday or trip that you have been putting off.
2. Start working on a side project or business idea.
3. Get some exercise and fresh air.
4. Eat healthily.
5. Take some time alone and do something that you like.
6. Spoil yourself with something "less healthy".
7. Spend time with friends and chat without an agenda.
8. Dream about your future. Think about where you want to be five-years' time.
9. Understand the impact that you can have on the lives of people when you are successful and enjoy what you are doing when you have the wind in your sails.
10. Watch that movie, eat chocolate and have some wine. Balance is key.

Final thought: If you enjoy your life, you will have more than enough energy to help others to enjoy theirs. First, be an example of how to live a wonderful life and then help others to do the same.

> *When you recover or discover something that nourishes your soul and brings joy, care enough about yourself to make room for it in your life.*

- Jean Shinoda Bolen

DEVELOP THE LEADER IN YOU

Leadership has nothing to do with us, but it has everything to do with the people around us. Leadership is not about me, it is always about you. Leadership is about developing those around you so they will succeed. Leadership is about cultivating leaders that can be better than ourselves. To be able to live a quality and fulfilling life we need to add value to the lives of people. If we only invest in ourselves, we are isolating ourselves from the world. We will have no place to share newfound insight or knowledge. We will be unable to understand the plight and hearts of people. Without action, empathy remains a word in a dictionary. The more we give the more we learn about ourselves. We can only develop emotionally if we interact with those around us. The more we understand people the more we will be able to understand ourselves.

> " *The task of the leader is to get his people from where they are to where they have not been.* "
>
> **- Henry Kissinger**

In his book, How to Win Friends and Influence People, Dale Carnegie has a treasure chest of advice on influence. The focus is on mobilising people to act and discover their hidden potential.

Six leadership principles from Dale Carnegie:

1. **Respect** – Show respect for peoples' opinion even if you don't agree. You will also never convince someone of anything if you don't respect them or their point of view.

2. **Admit** – Admit when you are wrong, and the right people will respect you. You will build on a foundation of honesty, integrity and respect. It will not always be easy, and the wrong kind of people will hold your mistakes against you and walk away. The right kind people will respect you and remain by your side.

3. **Questions** – Ask questions and give people a chance to answer. People will buy in when they feel heard and therefore respected. You cannot win people over by not listening to them and forcing your vision or opinion on them.

4. **Let them Speak** – People must be allowed to speak. It makes them feel that their opinion is valued and that they have something to contribute. If they feel that you value them by listening, they will be much more willing to listen to you.

5. **Understand** – We understand from our perspective. Only from putting yourself in the shoes of another person can we start to see from their point of view. Remember that you also only have a point of view. We only see the world through your eyes, and we need the eyes of others to broaden our view and to see the full picture. We don't know what we don't know, we are not the keeper of the absolute-truth or the master of all-insight.

6. **Challenge them** – People love a challenge and the opportunity to prove themselves. Giving people a challenge gives them a chance to excel. Be there to support them and to help them succeed.

Final thought: Don't just be a spectator in the leadership game, get onto the field and play the game.

> *Leadership is not about a title or a designation. It's about impact, influence and inspiration. Impact involves getting results, influence is about spreading the passion you have for your work, and you have to inspire team-mates and customers.*

- Robin S. Sharma

FIND YOUR COURAGE

We live in challenging times. Is our time more challenging than the times of those who came before us or those who will follow in our footsteps? I don't think so. The question is irrelevant because we are here now and we need to make things work, now. Our time here will always be challenging. Situations will change but challenges will remain. Courage is the decision to live your life on your terms. It's not about the big, bold actions but rather about small quality steps. Getting up after being knocked down by life. Courage is about a continuous positive movement in the face of fear. Courage is about not letting fear take control of our actions and dictate the way we live our lives. Courage is the decision to not allow ourselves to become spectators of life. Courage is the willingness to be an active player in the game of life. Courage is, embracing the value of the life we have, all the time working to have a positive impact on the world around us.

> " *I learned that courage was not the absence of fear, but the triumph over it. The brave man is not he who does not feel afraid, but he who conquers that fear.* "
>
> **- Nelson Mandela**

Fear is part of who we are. It is a defence mechanism that can keep us out of harm's way. Fear only becomes a problem if we allow it to control our lives. Fear becomes a problem if we base our decisions and actions on it rather than on the legacy we want for our lives.

Being courageous means to be strong enough in a moment to act. Courage is the act of standing up for those who cannot fight for themselves. Courage is not in this moment but in the next step you take. Courage is the action that flows from being strong, the action that moves you in the face of adversity. Courage is the action that gets you to where you want to go. The determination that keeps you on course. The resolve that gets you to your goal.

Being strong let you take the first step, being courageous let you take every step thereafter.

How can I find my courage? I use the following strategy to help me understand the challenge I face and to get me to act upon it.

1. **Find the source** – Understand why you fear something. Think about the impact it has on your life. Know why you need to address it.

2. **Act** – Your resolve must translate into action. Good ideas without action remain ideas. Ideas do not help people; ideas do not change the world. We change the world by acting.

3. **Understand the consequences of your inaction** – Understand what will happen if you do not act. Be aware of the ripple effect of your inaction. Know the impact of unaddressed fear on your life.

4. **Recognize the fear** – Accept that fear is a defence mechanism and part of who you are. It is there to help you make quality decisions. Do not make decisions based on fear but rather make decisions in the face of fear. Use fear as a mechanism which forces you to think twice and then make the right decision.

5. **Understand the "Who"** – Our decisions influence the world and people around us. Focus on the impact you want to make and the people you want to help.

6. **Communicate** – Talk to a trusted adviser or good friend about your fear. Get another perspective and advice. Even if someone just listens, it will help you organize your thoughts and come to terms with what needs to be done.

7. **Get inspired** – Always have the world you want to create, in mind. Be inspired by what you are striving to achieve, be motivated by the difference you want to make and the lives that you want to touch.

8. **Practice outside your comfort zone** – Doing things outside our comfort zones gets us used to the feeling of fear and help us to operate in the face of it. Every time I get to the top of a rock face or wall I climbed; my hands are shaking. I know that this is part of the journey and I am not going to stop because my mind is uncomfortable with the situation.

Final thought: You are much stronger than you think. The key to courage is, taking small steps and not stopping.

> *All you need is the plan, the road map, and the courage to press on to your destination.*
>
> **- Earl Nightingale**

DESIGN YOUR OPPORTUNITIES

In business, careers, sports and many other areas of our lives, we are constantly on the lookout for opportunities, opportunities that can take us to the next place on our journey. Opportunities that can lift us to the next level or catapult us to the front. We tend to see opportunities is a shortcut or Wormhole to where we want to be. Opportunities are neither an easy ride nor transportation to your final destination. Opportunities are the result of hard work, calculated risk, dedication, and perseverance.

It doesn't matter which way we slice it; without opportunities, we remain right where we are. A passive approach to opportunities i.e. waiting for opportunities is usually an ineffective strategy. The good news is that you are not at the mercy of others or sheer luck. People see opportunities as a passive stage where we are at the mercy of someone or something outside of our control, passengers waiting to arrive. This could not be further from the truth, an opportunity is just the result of an active, calculated and continuous process. Opportunities are a two-way street, a place where we have something to offer that someone else needs. A process where we refine our skills, build our brand and are actively exploring and understanding the world around us.

> *" We are all faced with a series of great opportunities brilliantly disguised as impossible situations. "*
>
> - Charles R. Swindoll

By actively investing in ourselves, contributing to society and understanding the needs of the world we live in, we can develop opportunities. This strategy not only creates opportunities for us but it will act as an opportunity incubator so that many more can benefit from our actions.

10 Ways to design your opportunities:

1. **Define the word** – Know what the word "opportunity" means to you. What do you expect to give and what do you expect to receive?

2. **Know your heading** – Any open door is not an opportunity. You need to know where you are headed and what you want to achieve. You need to differentiate between a viable opportunity that fits in with your vision and mission as opposed to a random opportunity which will lead you away from your passion, purpose and take away your joy.

3. **Know your ships** – Organizations and teams are just vessels in which people steer in the same direction to success or victory. You will not fit in everywhere because you are unique. Understand where you will fit in and where you will not. This will help you to narrow your focus, refine your search and to focus your energy and efforts in the right direction. Getting this right will save you a lot of time and heartache.

4. **Know your waters** – Where you search will have a lot to do with what you want to achieve. You have two options:

    - **Net fishing** - You put information out there or look everywhere to find something. This is a time consuming and ineffective process. Usually followed by people who lack in direction, goals and vision.

- **Spearfishing** - Here you look in specific places, target specific organizations, teams or people. You propose specific ideas, concepts and solutions. This is a focused and effective approach where you know your value and understand your environment.

5. **Know your uniqueness** – To be able to create opportunities, you need to understand your brand and your offering. You need to own your uniqueness and understand the value it holds. You need to be able to show how your brand will add value to any team, organization, or person that you collaborate with.

6. **Invest in yourself** – Don't stop learning or investing in your future because you got an opportunity, promotion or jumped to a specific level. If you want to be an opportunity incubator, you need to invest in your own growth and development, on a continuous basis. Learning, communicating, understanding, and contributing, will always be part of a purpose-driven life.

7. **Take the risk** – Risk and creativity go hand in hand. One cannot survive without the other. If you want to create opportunities, you need to take the risk and be creative. You must come up with extraordinary ideas, concepts, strategies, products, services or performances. You need to convey your message in a unique way to the right audience. It is a risk to put "The expeditionary" out there but without that risk, you and the world around you will remain exactly the way it is. The world develops because people take risks.

8. **Listen** – Keep on making contact with quality people. Listen to them and learn from them. Get their input and run your ideas and suggestions past them. Don't reinvent the wheel, rather have coffee with influential and successful people and

learn from their journeys. Get your name on their lips and your number on their phones.

9. **Ask** – Don't be afraid to ask for help, input, or advice. Discuss your suggestions and advice with quality people. This is the way you get to be the topic of discussions. Successful people usually love to give advice. Asking for advice is a way to spread the word about your brand.

10. **Be Agile** – To be able to capitalize on opportunities fast, you need to be in touch with what is happening around you. You need to adapt your strategy with the times. Supply something that is relevant and in short supply, today. Don't build a bridge where the river has dried up. Be relevant, move fast and adapt to a changing world.

Final thought: Don't wait for opportunities to appear, go out and create them. Create enough opportunities so that you don't need to travel alone. Become an opportunity incubator.

> *In every day, there are 1,440 minutes. That means we have 1,440 daily opportunities to make a positive impact.*
>
> **- Les Brown**

INVEST IN PEOPLE

John C. Maxwell calls it "The Law of Addition" and I call it, Investing in the Future. It doesn't matter what we call it, the principle remains: for the world to have a better tomorrow we need to build into the lives of people today. We need to make a selfless investment in the lives of people, without expecting a reward in return.

On second thought, this may not be true. When we invest in people we inevitably believe in the future. We believe in a better life for us and those whom we love. We believe in a brighter future and a better world. Not only a better future for the world we live in but also a brighter future for a world where we are mere memories. A world where the echoes of our silent voices are still whispering belief.

> *Too often we underestimate the power of a touch, a smile, a kind word, a listening ear, an honest compliment, or the smallest act of caring, all of which have the potential to turn a life around.*
>
> **- Leo Buscaglia**

Seven strategies to invest in people:

1. **Believe** – To be able to make a difference we need to believe in the person and in the future. Without these two beliefs we will find it very difficult to get close enough to anyone to make a lasting impact on their lives.

2. **Mentor** – Investing in people means that we need to cultivate a long-term relationship with them. A relationship where we can

make an impact over time. A relationship where we share our beliefs, experiences, failures and successes. A relationship where we share our highs and lows. A relationship where we are an active contributor with a positive outlook.

3. **Set the example** – We need to live our words and not only speak them. Success and failure are two concepts that need to be lived to be understood. If we can show people how to cope with failure and how to celebrate success, responsibly, we have gone a long way toward unlocking purpose-driven lives.

4. **Care** – Investing in people will always cost you something. Being willing to pay the price for caring will open the door to a deeper, more meaningful relationship.

5. **Pitch up** – Be there for the long term but also be available. When we invest in something, we don't only look at our investment at the end of the term, to see what happened to it. We keep a close eye on it and make adjustments as needed. We want to see it grow.

6. **Pick up** – We need to help those who have failed, those who are hopeless and those who hit rock bottom. That is where the real investment lies. Investing is an upward mindset.

7. **Celebrate** – Help people to succeed and then celebrate their successes with them. Take them from defeat to victory. Show them your recipe and make it possible for them to celebrate.

Final thought: We are not in this life to travel alone. Humans are supposed to travel together. The more we invest in each other the more precious our journey becomes.

> *Caring about others, running the risk of feeling, and leaving an impact on people, brings happiness.*
>
> **- Harold Kushner**

TOGETHER WE ARE BETTER

I have seen many times how the so-called underdogs of sport pulled of miraculous victories. Teams won while the odds were stacked against them. I have seen how fans and commentators stood speechless and in amazement of what just transpired. I have seen how teams with less money, talent, players and sponsorships still went and beat the best. How did they do it? They got one thing right.

They had synergy! Synergy can be defined as the combined power of a group of things when they are working together that is greater than the total power achieved by each working separately .

> *Synergy is better than my way or your way. It's our way.*
>
> **- Stephen Covey**

In other words, these teams knew exactly how to make the best use of what they had. Players worked together in an extraordinary way to achieve extraordinary results. Instead of having superstars, they had a Super Combined Effort.

10 Steps to achieve a Super Combined Effort:

1. A Common Goal which each team member understands and passionately buys in to.
2. Open, clear and effective communication on and off the field.
3. A solid and executable strategy where everyone knows their role and place.

4. Emotional intelligence to out-think and outsmart the opposition to swing the odds in your favour.
5. Responsibility for yourself, your role and your teammates.
6. Empathy for one another so that you can support each other when the pressure is on.
7. Determination to succeed no matter what the odds are.
8. An astonishing amount of Energy to give an above human effort.
9. Understand and respect the rules of the game. Use the rules to your advantage.
10. A love for the game!

Final thought: Together we are better, smarter, stronger and faster. Together we can achieve results that individuals cannot. Synergy is the vessel that transports us to places most people only dream about.

> *Synergy is what happens when one plus one equals ten or a hundred or even a thousand! It's the profound result when two or more respectful human beings determine to go beyond their preconceived ideas to meet a great challenge.*
>
> **- Stephen Covey**

RESOLVE CONFLICT AND FACILITATE SOLUTIONS

Conflict is all around us and an integral part of the world we live in. We live in a world where conflict is the norm and solutions are the exceptions. Human nature draws us towards finding differences rather than acknowledging similarities. We want to polarize, divide, and exclude. This puts us into a perpetual cycle of self-sabotage.

The origins of conflict can usually be found in three sources:
1. Selfishness
2. The Lust for power
3. Greed

There is however a fourth element that is far more prevalent than we like to acknowledge; fear. Fear makes people close ranks, shut down dialogue, become inflexible and unmovable. Fear stops progress and divides people. Fear generates problems and kills solutions.

> *Though force can protect in emergency, only justice, fairness, consideration and cooperation can finally lead men to the dawn of eternal peace.*
>
> **- Dwight D. Eisenhower**

Six consequences of stalemates and conflict:

1. **Opinions cast in stone** - In this mindset; I am right, and you are wrong and there is no room for discussion. I have insight and superior knowledge.

2. **A breakdown in communication** - Your point of view is wrong, irrelevant and carries no weight. Therefore, your words are meaningless, and I will not listen. I will also not try and explain myself.

3. **The determination to win all arguments** - We want to win arguments because we don't want to change, adapt or even be wrong. We want to be in control of the situation without exposing who we are. We know that we are vulnerable, and we don't want to advertise the fact.

4. **Rejection of different perspectives** - If we acknowledge that someone with a different perspective has a better point of view or even a better solution, then we need to admit that we don't have all the answers, we don't have the best perspective and we don't have the best insight into the situation. This way of thinking has its origin in a society where perfection and flawlessness are the benchmarks. We lose sight of the beauty of our imperfection and the amazing achievement through collaboration which brought us here. There is a theory that Homo Sapiens survives because we were the first to have language. We could communicate and collaborate to not only survive but to flourish. Communication united us and brought the best out of us. Together we became unstoppable.

5. **Rejection of the diversity of humanity and human thinking** - We are unique beings, each person is very different from the next. We look different, we think differently and we do differently. In

this lies the power of humanity, we make each other's strong by understanding each other's blind spots, weaknesses and looking out for one another. We are strong because we think differently from one another.

6. **Rejection of the power of diversity** - I am strong because you are different from me and therefore you make me strong. I can take comfort in the notion that you see what I don't see and that you know what I don't know. Together we are smarter, stronger, and faster.

To be able to grow as humans and expand our knowledge we should lose arguments. Losing arguments means that we are open to listening, open to diverse opinions, open to change and in constant search of better solutions. It means that we are not bigger than the picture, we are just paint on a brush.

> " *Competition has been shown to be useful up to a certain point and no further, but cooperation, which is the thing we must strive for today, begins where competition leaves off.* "
>
> **- Franklin D. Roosevelt**

10 Strategies to resolve stalemates and conflict:

1. **Set boundaries** – Set out the rules of the conflict resolution game. Things like; no personal attacks. Focus on the issue at hand. No one is right, and no one is wrong. We want to find a solution to benefit all.

2. **Location** – Take people out of the situation to a neutral place, outside of their physical comfort zones. A place where no one has the high ground in terms of comfort.

3. **Find a common goal** – Where are we headed, what do we want to achieve and how will this benefit both parties? If we can aim at a goal that is close to all of us, we will be much more open and willing to move past the stalemates and make sacrifices, so that we can reach our goals.

4. **Conflict will happen** – Understand that conflict is a normal part of life and conflict in some way, shape or form, happens daily. The way we resolve conflict is what distinguishes us from the rest. It is what makes us successful or not.

5. **Listen to hear something new** – We must remove preconceived ideas and our ego's, out of listening. We need to try and hear the heart of what someone is saying. We need to find the message without the clutter of our noise. Turn down your radio and listen to someone else's composition.

6. **Mutual Respect** – If we don't have and show respect, we will not resolve conflict. We don't need to like one another, but we can treat each other with respect. Treating people with respect opens doors and unlocks leniency as well as the willingness to find solutions.

7. **How can I make you successful?** – Contemplate about how you can get the best for the other person out of this situation. We must ask ourselves, what is the best we can do for the person? By doing this we are already winning because we are taking control and responsibility for the situation. We are becoming accountable.

8. **Find the quality in the person** – Identify the qualities you like about the person and tell it to them. Let them understand that you see more in them than just this conflict or stalemate. Make sure that they understand that you see the human in them.

9. **Compromise** – Facilitate a win-win outcome, not a win-lose situation. Be ready to give something up to be able to move forward. A step back can often be the best way to move forward.

10. **Summarize what you hear** – Ensure that you understand what the other person is saying. An effective way of doing this is to repeat it in your own words i.e. I hear you are saying ... Is that correct or am I missing part of your message?

Final thought: More people must become conflict-resolution facilitators so that we can enable society to overcome prejudice, fear, and division. We must enable society to move effectively into the future by empowering people to cooperate and to find mutually beneficial solutions for a diverse world. We need to show people that, together we are better.

> " *No leader, however strong, can succeed at anything of national importance or significance unless he has the support and cooperation of the people he is tasked to lead and sworn to serve.* "
>
> **- Rodrigo Duterte**

PART 5:
CULTIVATE YOUR HABITS

DESIGN HABITS FOR SUCCESS

Habits might be small, but they have an enormous impact on our lives. With your habits, you are not only touching your life but also the lives of those around you. You are shaping your future and lighting up theirs.

> *The secret to habits can be found in simplicity and consistency. Just do and repeat.*
>
> **– Lourens Botha**

At some stage in my life, I got to a point where I had enough of the same. I knew I wanted to change, even more so, I had to change. I wanted the life I was dreaming about. The first change I made was adding quality habits to my daily routine. After a while of doing these small things, I realized that I was repeating the same things each day because I found value in them. Quality habits are always available, and it is our choice whether we use them to become what we dream about or not use them and stay where we are. I knew, by adding one habit to my routine was probably not going to win me the Nobel Prize. Still, one habit, as part of an arsenal of quality habits, will get me back on track and on my way to the life I wanted.

After listening to the advice of John C. Maxwell, in Orlando, U.S.A., some years ago, I realised the importance of adopting quality habit from successful people.

Four habits I adopted from John C. Maxwell are:

1. **Read** – Quality material that adds value to your life. I have long ago bought into this concept, and it is part of my personal development strategy. I read books, articles, blogs and quotes to inspire me, to gain knowledge and to grow as a person.

2. **Think** – How can I use this new information in my life? This helps me to make the information and concepts part of my life and incorporate it into my life-strategy. Whether I build it into my daily routine, develop a business plan or use it to enhance the lives of others, I get to put the written words into action.

3. **Write** – Write down any ideas, plans, insight, and creativeness that you come up with. It did not take me long to realize that if I don't write down my ideas, they will be lost forever. I make use of a notebook in which I can write my ideas immediately. Sometimes months go by and then I read through my notes and find an idea that was not applicable before but that I can use now.

4. **Ask** – We need to make use of our opportunities to ask quality questions to quality people. By quality questions, I mean questions of which the answer will help you to build quality not only into your life but also into the lives of those around you. This is one of the areas where most people fail. We don't ask questions anymore. Most people work in organizations and are surrounded by a world of knowledge and expertise. Yet we choose to struggle on our own, trying to reinvent the wheel, making mistakes that have already been made. I make it a point to make contact with people and ask questions. I want to learn.

Final thought: Habits must be practised daily, that is why they are called habits. When quality habits become part of our lives, it takes us on a wonderful journey.

> *"You'll never change your life until you change something you do daily. The secret of your success is found in your daily routine."*
>
> **– John C. Maxwell**

OWN YOUR ATTITUDE

You cannot control life, but you can control your attitude towards life. If you seek to find beauty, love, happiness, quality, and growth, then that is exactly what you will find. In striving to find these values, you will inadvertently carry those values into the world. By subscribing to these values, we are already making them part of who we are, part of our presence, our offering, and our brand. People will see these qualities and values in you before you even say a word. You will become what you seek. Our attitude is determined by what we are looking for. If we are looking to find the positive and the inspirational, our attitude to life becomes positive and we become inspired and become an inspiration to others.

> *If you don't like something, change it.*
> *If you can't change it, change your attitude.*
>
> **- Maya Angelou**

When I got into private practice, I knew it was going to take some time to get my business up and running. Most of the experts and entrepreneurs I spoke to told me that it would probably take me between three and five years to establish my name and my brand. Instinctively, I knew that the next 36 months, at least was going to be challenging. However, I did not get discouraged because I was determined to be successful and reach my goal. I had no plans to turn around and go back. For me, there was only one direction and that was forward.

During this period, I made a couple of really good decisions, and I also made some really bad ones. One specific decision laid the foundation for my success. I knew I had to stay positive and that my attitude would determine my success. I decided to bombard myself with positive input and inspiring material. I started reading quotes, books, articles, verses and blogs to inspire me. I read the success stories of people and used their success to inspire me. I used their strategies to enhance my strategies. I started writing on social media not only to inspire myself but also to inspire those around me. Sure enough, it gave me the results I needed. My attitude about life, people, adversity, and success changed. I started looking at the world, time, and purpose in a whole new way. I was on my way to becoming the man I always wanted to be (not there yet but working hard at it).

> *Choosing to be positive and having a grateful attitude is going to determine how you're going to live your life.*
>
> **- Joel Osteen**

Six questions to help you to examine your attitude:
1. What do I want to get out of life?
2. What do I want to bring to life?
3. Who oversees my thoughts and my actions?
4. What do I read?
5. To whom do I listen?
6. What is my agenda?

Final thought: Attitude is a choice. It is the process of taking responsibility for our thoughts which flow into our actions. Taking responsibility to influence ourselves and steer us towards who we want to be. Habits empower us to become a better version of ourselves.

> *Attitude is a lifelong journey in which we have a choice of destination.*
>
> **– Lourens Botha**

FIND MEANING IN THE CHAOS

When we go through adversity it feels like the world has moved on and we were left behind. Everyone has a purpose and a place to be, except us. It feels like we have fallen through the cracks of life. People around us continue with their lives, doing the same things which they have always done. We are left to wonder, do we still belong, do we still matter? While it seems that for everyone else it is business as usual, we are stuck in limbo. You, my friend, are in uncharted territory and your heading is unknown. Your ship is in open water and there is no port in sight. You are a true explorer of life, living without a map.

> *I will love the light for it shows me the way, yet I will endure the darkness because it shows me the stars.*
>
> **- Og Mandino**

You are walking through fire and your predictable life is gone. Every day presents you with uncharted waters, new trials, and the challenge to get up and face uncertainty. You have received telling blows from life and are struggling to find your feet. Your security has been ripped from under you, your anchor chain cut, and you are adrift at sea. Your world has been ripped from under your feet.

You are not in the cracks of life or at the back of the queue. Actually, you are in front, discovering a new trail, making a new way so that someone can follow safely in your footsteps. You are lighting up an unknown path, a path that many will be forced to walk. If would have been easy, we would not be talking about it. You are walking through fire and just by getting up every morning and by continuing you are doing what many, can't. You are a trail-blazer.

Keep in mind:

1. You are not alone. Many people are going through adversity and have to deal with serious setbacks.
2. This journey is leading you to a better place. Things will get better with time.
3. You need to get up every morning. Keep moving so that you can get through this. You are making a way where there is none.
4. Learn from where you are now. Become smarter, wiser, stronger and more prepared for the future.
5. Revisit your goals. Make sure your goals are still relevant and that they still inspire you. Remember that you are growing, and your goals will change.
6. The most successful people had to go through adversity before they became successful. Adversity has nothing to do with who you are, but it has everything to do with who you become.
7. Don't compare yourself to anyone. You are unique and so is your journey. You are living a very unique adventure that in future, you will tell unique stories about.
8. Revisit your priorities. Adversity teaches us that what used to be important isn't necessarily important, anymore. You are changing and growing all the time. Confirm to yourself what you see as important in your life and then let the outdated stuff go.
9. brace your new life. You are doing things differently now. Your schedule and priorities have changed. Don't hold on to what

was. You are in a new place. Emigrate your mind to this new place and live here. Find the value in the uniqueness of the place where you are now.

10. Know that you don't need to be at a specific place, space or stage in your life today. Your journey is unique and so are you. You are where you are and that is life.

Final thought: You are on your way to a new future. Embrace today and find the magic.

> *" The best preparation for tomorrow is doing your best today. "*
>
> **- H. Jackson Brown, Jr.**

FIND PURPOSE IN PATIENCE

We live in a highly pressurised society. Very view things that happen around us is not happening under or because of pressure. If we do not perform in relation to the pressure put on us, we fall through the cracks, get left behind or are just discarded. If we do not react "applicable" to pressure, we do not make the cut and therefore we can be seen as insignificant.

The American Indians has a wonderful saying about patience and living a unique lifestyle. They say, *"You dance to the beat of a different drum."*

> *Each life is made up of mistakes and learning, waiting and growing, practising patience and being persistent.*
>
> **- Billy Graham**

In order to cope we adapt a Perform-to-please mindset. We try to relieve these pressures by meeting the expectations of those applying it. This strategy will however soon present its own set of problems. You will burn yourself out trying to please everyone. The result will probably be you getting discarded and someone else replacing you. I am not even mentioning the emotional, physical, psychological and relationship damage that this type of Perform-to-please mindset, does to people.

The next mindset is one where we want to achieve our goals and dreams yesterday. I call it the: No-tomorrow mindset. In this mindset, we always see ourselves as way behind where we should be. We do this in terms of our growth, potential and lives. We put an enormous amount of pressure on ourselves to "catch up". The sad part is that in the minds of these individuals they will never catch up and the pressure will never be relieved. This mindset leaves us with feelings of emptiness, regret, and, also being uninspired. In both mindsets, we find ourselves living unfulfilled and empty lives. In both mindsets, we are dancing to the beat of someone else's drum.

Being different and living at a different pace means we need to view every day as unique. We need to design our lives so that you can be who you are but also who you want to become. We need to find our unique place in the puzzle.

10 Principles to cultivate patience in your life:

1. **Recognize your Impatience** – The moment we acknowledge that we are impatient it liberates us. We can only address a problem if we acknowledge it. Accept that you can only do so much, and you are not going to change the world in a day. You can change the day for yourself.

2. **Embrace Discomfort** – Accept discomfort as one of the characteristics that come with a purpose-driven life. When we live with purpose and have dreams and goals, we always have pressure pulling us towards them. We want to achieve and just by wanting to achieve we are already achieving. Remember that you are the master of your Achievement-pressure, not the other way round. You dictate the pace.

3. **Life is outside your Comfort Zone** – We were not created for a life of comfort, and that is exactly why we don't grow and excel inside

our comfort zones. Don't mistake the discomfort of a purpose-driven life with the pressures of society. This pressure has a purpose but the responsibility to manage it effectively remains on us.

4. **Life is turbulent** – Things will not always go your way. Accept it and rather focus on finding what is "going your way". Find the value in your life and focus your attention on it. This is where you will probably find your purpose as well.

5. **Focus on your Goal** – By always keeping an eye on our vision for our life we can rate and rank all other pressure. Be aware that you are all the time moving towards your goals, the pace might vary but you are still moving forward. We need to decide whether the pressure is relevant or not. Keep in mind that there is no success without pain and sacrifice but the pressure you experience must always pull you towards your dreams and goals. If not, you need to revaluate the specific pressure.

6. **Motivate Yourself** – Use the pressure to catapult you towards your goals. Positive and inspired pressure will always lead to growth. The pressure you endure should motivate you because it is an indicator that you are en route to where you want to be. Pressure should not be in vain; it has to have a purpose.

7. **Build Character** – Remind yourself that positive pressure and time spent, are part of a process making you stronger and building your character. It builds the character that you will need when you achieve your goals. There will be all-new pressure on you when you achieve goals, the pressure and the press for time will not disappear.

8. **Self-Talk** – The way we talk to ourselves determines if we will be successful or not. Tell yourself that you are worth the sacrifice

and time spent. Tell yourself that you are growing all the time. Tell yourself that a beautiful future awaits you and that future started yesterday.

9. **Recognize your uniqueness** – You are moving at your own pace because you are unique and so is your journey. You can schedule your time, but you cannot control Life. Don't compare your journey to those of others. You are discovering a new life, not imitating someone else's.

10. **Life is not a race** – There is no specific time and date for you to arrive at your goals and dreams. You need to live your dreams, not reach them.

Final thought: There is no blueprint for the life you want, no map to outline your journey. You are a ship sailing in uncharted waters. Your destination is not the purpose of the journey. Your purpose is to discover as you explore. Your purpose is to love your journey while you live one day at a time.

> " *Never cut a tree down in the wintertime. Never make a negative decision in the low time. Never make your most important decisions when you are in your worst moods. Wait. Be patient. The storm will pass. The spring will come.* "
>
> **- Robert H. Schuller**

CHASE SERENDIPITY

The result we envision when starting something has a direct impact on the success we achieve. The outcome we envision will determine the way we approach what we do. To take it one step further; the word SERENDIPITY speaks about the belief that everything will turn out right in the end. The belief that things will work in your favour.

Why is this important? It is important because, to be successful, we need to believe in what we do. We must believe in the result we are aiming for. By going through the motions of doing something we do not believe in, we set ourselves up for failure. If we believe that everything will end well, we take the pressure out of the situation. We give ourselves breathing space and room to move. It is in this space where we find our creativity, where we discover new insights and ideas. It is in this space where we discover almost unlimited inspiration and energy. Why? Because in our minds we are headed for victory and success. Even more, we are living the victory before we achieve it.

> " *Keep your dreams alive. Understand to achieve anything requires faith and belief in yourself, vision, hard work, determination, and dedication. Remember all things are possible for those who believe.* "
>
> **- Gail Devers**

Five questions to help you discover Serendipity:

1. **Why?** – Why are you doing this? Make sure that you have a strong motive or reason for doing something. Understand why you are doing it. Take the uncertainty out of the reason.

2. **How?** – Understanding how you are going to achieve a result, will give you direction, purpose and momentum. Empower yourself by knowing what your next step should be. Take the uncertainty out of the road to travel.

3. **When?** – Commit yourself to timelines. This will keep you accountable in terms of your progress and the time you allocated to achieve your goal. Getting this right will prevent you from losing interest or momentum. Take the uncertainty out of the timeline.

4. **Who?** – By involving quality people in the process, you multiply your chances for success. Involve people who can keep you accountable and on-track. Involve people who can guide, motivate, advice and who can keep you informed. Involve people who can cover your blind spots. Take the uncertainty out of the unknown.

5. **Where?** – Define the outcomes you are looking for. Understand where you want to end up. What should the place where you are headed, look like. If we can see the result, understand it and express it, we can build it. Take the uncertainty out of the result.

Final thought: The key is not to stress or get distracted by factors outside our control. We can only do what we can do and that is exactly what we need to do. Let the rest go and believe in the result.

> *We have always held to the hope, the belief, the conviction that there is a better life, a better world, beyond the horizon.*

- Franklin D. Roosevelt

THE KEYS TO A REMARKABLE LIFE

PART 6:

DESIGN YOUR STRATEGY FOR LIFE

TAKE A CALCULATED RISK

Staying where you are is a much greater risk than taking a step into the unknown. We owe it to ourselves to take the risk to get yourself to a better place. To take the risk and live a quality life where you can become a better version of yourself. If you don't take a risk and stay where you are, you will probably regret it later on.

> " We must all suffer one of two things: the pain of discipline or the pain of regret or disappointment. "
>
> - Jim Rohn

Three factors influence our appetite for risk:

- **Fear** – The fear of the unknown and fear of failure.
- **Comfort** – In your mind, your comfort zone is more appealing than anything the future might hold.
- **Ignorance** – You are unaware of your unlimited potential and where it can take you.

Both these factors will rob you of a fulfilling and meaningful life. If you give in to one or both of them, chances are good that you will get to the end of your life with a backpack filled with regrets.

10 Ways to step out of your comfort zone:

1. Do something that scares you and celebrate you pushing your boundaries.

2. Visualize what your life can be like if you stepped out of your comfort zone. Dream big dreams and get excited about what the future might hold.
3. Write down what is important to you and build your new life on that foundation.
4. Think of how you want to be remembered. Take control of your life story.
5. Listen to your inner voice. You know what your dreams and aspirations are.
6. Change one thing in your daily routine and add one new habit each month.
7. Get some fresh air and exercise. Take care of your mind and body.
8. Ask advice from someone who has been there and overcame the "slump".
9. Get your motivation by acknowledging the pain regret already caused you.
10. Make a list of the steps you need to put in place to change your life.

Final thought: Do not let regret be your last emotion. Grab onto life and live your adventure.

> *" We live in a wonderful world that is full of beauty, charm and adventure. There is no end to the adventures that we can have if only we seek them with our eyes open. "*
>
> **- Jawaharlal Nehru**

GET UP ONE MORE TIME

Life has given all of us some telling blows. We have taken shots left, right, centre, fair and unfair and yet, here we are. How is that even possible in such a volatile and unpredictable world? It is possible because you chose to get up more times than you got knocked down. Even if it is just one more time. By getting up, you not only showed guts, determination, and strength, you also showed that you understand one of the secrets of success and life. The secret of not letting anything keep you down because you value your life and the time you have.

> *We all have dreams. But in order to make dreams come into reality, it takes an awful lot of determination, dedication, self-discipline, and effort.*
>
> **- Jesse Owens**

In 1968 Tanzanian long-distance runner, John Stephen Akhwari travelled to the Olympic games in Mexico City. His aim was to win an Olympic gold medal for his country in the marathon. From the start of the race, Akhwari had difficulties with the altitude. From early in the race he started cramping up. He was determined to get into a better position and ran through the pain. Just before halfway he was involved in a pile-up, fell, and ended up with cuts, bruises, and a dislocated knee. Akhwari did not stop. He continued to do what he set out. He crossed the finish line more than an hour after the winner.

When asked after the race, why he did not stop, his answer was: "My country did not send me 5,000 miles to start the race, they sent me 5,000 miles to finish the race."

> *The price of success is hard work, dedication to the job at hand, and the determination that whether we win or lose, we have applied the best of ourselves to the task at hand.*
>
> **- Vince Lombardi**

12 Tips to help you to continue your journey:

1. Don't be a hostage of your past. Learn from your past and enter your future with experience.

2. Don't allow the low expectations others have for your life, to hold you back. You have unlimited potential. Believe it and live courageously.

3. Don't let false perceptions, gossip or untrue stories keep you down. Choose to tell your own story and don't let anyone dictate what story you should tell.

4. Don't wait for others to buy into your dreams before you start chasing them. They are your dreams and you chase them because you believe in them, and that is enough.

5. Don't expect people to agree with your goals or your journey. Your goals are your goals, and your journey is your journey. Keep them sacred, nourish them and pursue them with authority and determination.

6. Don't allow anyone to determine or dictate your future or goals. You choose your own goals and you hunt them down.

7. Don't allow failure to stop you and keep you down. Everyone fails but only a few have the courage to get up and continue. These men and women are the few who will succeed.

8. Fight for what you believe in and carve a future out of the rock you chose.

9. Know that you only have one life here and that you are the only one that can make it count.

10. Believe that you can still make a difference in your own life but also in the lives of others.

11. Believe that better days are on the way and you just need to weather the storm. Remember: every storm runs out of water at some point.

12. Believe in yourself and your potential. Know that you matter.

Final thought: Live your life on your terms. Make sure that only the right people can speak into your life. Filter out the noise of the rest, you do not need it.

> *Keep your dreams alive. Understand to achieve anything requires faith and belief in yourself, vision, hard work, determination, and dedication. Remember all things are possible for those who believe.*
>
> **- Gail Devers**

CAPTAIN THE SHIP

Going through adversity is not bestowed on a selected few. We all go through adversity at some point and surely not once, only. Setbacks are part of our existence here on earth. It is not the exception but more likely, the rule. When I go through challenging times and struggle to make sense of what is going on or why things are happening the way they are, I always think about the last scene in Pirates of the Caribbean: Dead Man's chest. The words spoken by Naomie Harris (Tia Dalma) go something like this: "If you are willing to brave the haunted shores of Worlds-end then you will need a captain that knows those waters."

> *It is the set of the sails, not the direction of the wind that determines which way we will go.*
>
> **- Jim Rohn**

Whenever I go through tough times, I always tell myself that this is preparing me to be the captain of someone's ship and navigate them through uncharted waters. I must gain experience if I want to play a role in the lives of others. How do we sail Uncharted Waters? We can learn a lot from how the early seafaring nations explored uncharted waters.

Eight strategies early explorers used to sail uncharted waters:
1. **Course** – They always had a goal and a purpose. Whether it was to find new trade routes or new merchandise to trade, they knew exactly what they wanted to achieve. When we go through

adversity, we need to keep an eye on where we are heading with our lives. Knowing what we still want to do or achieve will help to pull us forward and give us direction.

2. **Strong ships** – They built their ships from the best timber they could find, and they took care of it. By caring for what we have, we find value and purpose in our lives.

3. **Loyalty** – They appointed a loyal crew. By travelling with people who knows where you are headed and what you are going through help to keep us going and gives us direction.

4. **Skills** – They appointed skilled people. By looking at, listening to and learning from skilled people, we can make life easier for ourselves. We don't need to reinvent the wheel.

5. **They measured wind speed to determine the distance travelled** – If we can keep track of our progress and celebrate even the slightest movement forward, we can motivate ourselves to keep going.

6. **Basic navigation for direction** – They used basic navigation instruments very effectively. They understood the limitations of what they had but made the most of it anyway. "If we make the most of what we have, we will soon have what we want most." – Unknown author.

7. **Patience** – They did not know when they would reach land, so they had patience. They lived day by day. If we live for today and find quality in today, we take the pressure off tomorrow.

8. **Weathered the storms** – Not knowing what will happen next, they handled every situation as it arose. We want to "handle" everything all at once. If we take care of what is pertinent at this moment, we will be able to cope and not be overwhelmed by everything else.

Final thought: We cannot live in fear if we want to sail uncharted waters. We need to decide what takes preference in our minds. Limit the impact of fear on your life by being determined to sail where no man has sailed and to discover life on your terms.

> *Following the light of the sun, we left the Old World.*
>
> **- Christopher Columbus**

ASSEMBLE YOUR INNER CIRCLE

In his book, The 21 Irrefutable Laws of Leadership, John C. Maxwell, talks about, the Law of the inner circle. He explains why it is so difficult to be successful when we travel alone. In order to be successful, we need people to support, advise, motivate and inspire us. In my view the inner circle as a small group of between 3 and 5 people who will journey with you and help you to be successful. People who understand your passion know your dreams but most of all, people who understand your weak points. These are the people that will give you an honest opinion, keep you accountable, grow with you and pick you up when you fall or fail. These are the people who want to see you succeed.

> *Love is friendship that has caught fire.*
> *It is quiet understanding, mutual*
> *confidence, sharing and forgiving. It is*
> *loyalty through good and bad times.*
> *It settles for less than perfection and makes*
> *allowances for human weaknesses.*
>
> **– Ann Landers**

The smart thing to do when putting an Inner Circle in place is to find people who think a bit different, people who look at life from a different angle. These are the type of people who will be able to see your Blind Spots and who will help you compensate for those. If we all think the same, speak the same and do the same, we are not growing; we are disappearing.

We need strong quality people who open our horizons. The responsibility is on us to communicate the role we want these people to play in our lives. The difficult thing is to give your Inner Circle the authority to speak into your life. It is a bold, liberating and very necessary step. You will only be able to do this successfully if you have a Growth Mindset. With a Growth Mindset, knowledge, truth, and growth are much more important than ego.

Your Inner Circle also becomes your "Criticism Filter". Because you live outside your comfort zone and sail uncharted waters, you need to take risks, do unconventional things and live your life in a unique way. This will inevitably lead to you being criticized by people from outside. You can discuss criticism with you Inner Circle, and they can help you to identify what is relevant and help you make the necessary changes but even more important, they can help you let go of the other stuff, the noise people make.

> *You will never reach your destination if you stop and throw stones at every dog that barks.*
>
> ### - Winston Churchill

People like Steve Jobs, Richard Branson, Bill Gates and Jeff Bezos showed us that risk and failure are all part of the journey to success. You cannot be successful without taking risks. I say again: Risk and Failure are packed together and stored on the same shelf, high-up and at the back. Only the brave will intentionally reach for them, knowing that they go together.

Seven criteria for an inner circle:

1. **Blind spots** – I choose my inner circle based on my weaknesses, flaws and blind spots. Because I am a dominant right-brain thinker, the majority of my Inner Circle are strong Left-brain thinkers.

2. **Buy-In** – I only include people if they buy into my vision, goals and the legacy I want to leave. I want to get to my goal, not explain the entire way why I am going there. Everyone must be focused on the same result. They want to see me succeed and will do everything in their power to get me to the finish line, even drag me across the line.

3. **Honesty** – I don't need people who will tell me what I want to hear. I need people who can give me an honest answer without trying to please me. I want to move forward, not strengthen my ego. Telling me that I am on track will not help me avoid the oncoming freight train.

4. **Only a Few** – My inner circle never consists of more than five people. If everybody is part of your inner circle, it is not an inner circle, it is a crowd. It will lead to a situation where only those who shout the loudest, will be heard.

5. **Availability** – I need people who are available to help me make decisions as they arise, people who will be there to assist me in averting a crisis or grabbing hold of an opportunity. If a person can only talk to you once every two weeks, then they will not fit the profile. (Keep in mind that a person can be trusted advisors even though they are not part of your inner circle.) Do not neglect quality people because you chose an inner circle. An inner circle is not a club, it is a vessel to help you reach your goals.

6. **Accountability** – I need people who will make sure I do what I said I would. People who will help me make deadlines and stick to my schedule. People who will help me get there in time and on time.

7. **Track Record** – I need people with proven success track records. People who know about risk, failure, success. People who know how to build a legacy.

Final thought: What your inner circle does for you, you must do for them. You are also part of their inner circle, invited or not. That is your legacy. Who is your inner circle, and do they know it?

> *" The strong bond of friendship is not always a balanced equation; friendship is not always about giving and taking in equal shares. Instead, friendship is grounded in a feeling that you know exactly who will be there for you when you need something, no matter what or when. "*
>
> **- Simon Sinek**

UNLOCK YOUR EMOTIONAL INTELLIGENCE

The experiences of life remain constant, the decision to learn from them and become smarter is a choice. I have seen many intelligent people not amount to much in their lifetimes. I kept on questioning this phenomenon. Is success not a given when intelligence is present? After thinking long and hard about this phenomenon I concluded that to be successful we must have Emotional Intelligence (EQ). Being intelligent but unable to apply intelligence in a rapid moving, fast-evolving, and agile world, will probably not amount to success. For humans to be successful we need to understand the world we live in. For us to be smarter than the game, we must understand the rules of the game. If we understand the rules, we can use it in our favour.

> " *Emotional Intelligence is: Understanding the rules of the game, knowing yourself and having the ability to use both in your favour.* "
>
> **– Lourens Botha**

Emotional Intelligence is not a hidden mystery of life. There are more than enough research and knowledge out there to get us going.

13 Areas of emotional intelligence I focused on:

1. **Robust emotional vocabulary** – I had an extremely limited emotional vocabulary, probably a "man thing". I wanted to understand my emotions so that I could take control. If I can articulate what I'm feeling, then I can probably identify the source

of my emotions. If I can identify the source of the emotion, then I can come up with a plan to address it or just accept emotions for what they are and move on with my life.

2. **Control your thoughts** – One of the most powerful tools in our armour is our ability to control and focus our thoughts. We have a choice to focus on the positive, on the future, on growth, success and joy. We can steer our thoughts away from the negative to the positive. However, the "ability" to do something does not imply that we do it. We need to consciously steer away from negative thoughts. It takes time to become a habit. Stay with it, it is worth your patience.

3. **Know yourself** – We cannot embark on a journey of growth if we are not honest about who we are. We need to know our strengths and weaknesses. By acknowledging our weaknesses, we empower ourselves a chance to work on them and develop ourselves. Knowing your strengths will help you find your purpose, passion and create a vision for your life.

4. **Learn from criticism** – For most of us, criticism is one of those things that we would rather avoid. We see it as an assault on the very essence of who we are. There are a couple of things we can do with criticism:

    - Evaluate, who it is coming from. If it is from a person that you respect, you can try and learn something from it. If it comes from someone that you don't respect or who don't respect you, you leave it there. If we let everybody have a say in our lives, it's not our lives anymore.

    - Ask yourself if it is criticism or advice? Advice is solution-focused and growth generating. Advice has the best for you in mind. Take the advice and build it into your strategy and move on. If it is criticism, try to understand where the origin is. Is there something you must change, work on or maybe approach differently?

5. **Demonstrate empathy** – Find people within their situation, understand what they are going through not because you have been through the same but because you care. Empathy is more about our availability to people than it is about exactly understanding what they are going through. Can people depend on us and are we available? Do we listen or do we judge?

6. **Give praise** – We all love to receive praise but few of us are equipped to give praise. On the other hand, very few of us are equipped to receive praise. Rather than an ego boost, praise is an indication that we are on track with what we set out to accomplish. Praise is a habit that can be developed. Start by giving praise to those closest to you and see how they start to bloom. The more we give praise the less we expected it. Giving praise is an inseparable part of Growth and Leadership mindsets. Praise is about lifting people, giving them confidence and empowering them to succeed.

7. **Don't dwell on the past** – Learning from our mistakes is one of the most powerful things Emotional Intelligent people do. Emotional Intelligent people are agile, they learn from the past, adapt, change behaviour, and move on. We cannot change the past, it is there to learn from, not to live in.

8. **Admit mistakes** – By admitting our mistakes we make ourselves strong, build quality relationships and empower ourselves to become more successful. We are teaching ourselves to learn from our mistakes rather than fearing them.

9. **See people for who they are, not for who you are** – We evaluate people on who we are and not on who they are and what they do. If they do what we do or what we expect them to do, we easily find quality in them. If they do things differently, we usually come up with criticism. Evaluate people on the grounds of the value they give and the impact they make, not in terms of the way they do it.

10. **Avoid dream killers** – Dream Killers are those people who do not believe in you or your dreams, those people who do not want you to succeed. Your failure is their success. Cut them out of your life and move on. Do not make a big thing about it, just move on. They are not worth your energy.

11. **Adapt and be agile** – We can only see what we can see, we only know what we know, and we don't know what we don't know. What seemed impossible yesterday becomes possible today because we can learn, grow, gain experience and adapt. Just like an aeroplane adjusting its course to get to its destination, so we must be able to adapt by using newfound knowledge, experience, and information. We are all the time refining the end-product of what we want to be or where we want to be. We should constantly evaluate the world around us, all the time in search of insight and opportunities. As creative beings, we cannot afford to get stuck with a past version of our reality. Do not hold yourself hostage in past ways but embrace the opportunities that come with change.

12. **Become future-focused** – Keep your focus on the future. Everything you do today will have a ripple effect on your future. What you do today will shape your future. Measure everything you do to the future you want. If what you do enhance the future you want, then keep on doing it. If not, let it go. By looking at

the future, we keep ourselves accountable for what we are doing today. We live with purpose.

13. **Disconnect** – We all need "Time off the grid". Time to recharge and to get energized. It doesn't matter if you do it alone or with friends or family. It can be on your bed reading a book while hiking in the hills. The where and when is irrelevant and dependent on your unique being. The only thing that matters is that you make time to disconnect from your phone, social media, the work or anything that drains your energy.

Final thought: Success cannot be defined in only one way. Every person has a different understanding of what success is. Don't use the success-script handed to you by society. Define success in your own words according to your being and on your terms. I urge you to do three things when you define your success: Be grateful, be gentle and be unique.

> " *No doubt emotional intelligence is more rare than book smarts, but my experience says it is actually more important in the making of a leader. You just can't ignore it.* "
>
> **- Jack Welch**

BECOME RESILIENT

I always try and learn something from those people who became extraordinary in their fields. More so, those who managed to remain at the "Top" for more than just a moment. When we look at the most successful people in business and sport, we find some interesting phenomena. Talent can take you to the top fast, but it will not keep you there. IQ can do the same, but it will not cement your place at the top. In business and sport, it is not the smartest or the most talented who remains at the top. It is those who are more resilient, more adaptable, more agile, and more street-smart than the rest. It is those who get up the most times after being knocked down. It is the resilient.

> *You're going to go through tough times – that's life. But I say, 'Nothing happens to you, it happens for you.' See the positive in negative events.*
>
> **- Joel Osteen**

Mental toughness is one of those things that some people are born with, while others need to develop it over time. You can develop mental toughness through your circumstances or by learning and applying the skills needed to be resilient. No matter how you become resilient, it will cost you something. Like leadership skills, mental toughness skills can be adopted and become a part of your life.

Being resilient will equip you to look at the world, adversity, and opportunities, in an entirely new way. It will not only equip you with the resilience and determination to get up when you run into the "wall" but it will also help you find the holes in the "walls of life".

Here are a few things you can work on to increase your Mental Toughness:

1. **The Price** – Everything we want in life has a price. Make sure you are willing to pay that price. If you are willing to pay the price, the will to continue in the face of adversity will drive you to success.

2. **The Goal** – If we focus on a specific goal we can get through the most challenging times. Our goals are ropes that pull us out of our current reality and into a world of possibilities. I call this my Grappling hook theory.

3. **Self-Talk** – Become your own best friend. Let your inner voice be positive, caring, and inspirational. If you get this right, your actions will start to imitate your inner voice.

4. **See Failure is an opportunity** – Lower the value of failure and increase the value of Risk. Rather learn something out of every situation than not trying at all. Failure allows us to become smarter, stronger, more experienced and to come up with a better strategy. Failure is an opportunity to regroup and come back stronger.

5. **Body Language** – Even if you feel like staying down, get up, dress up and look the part. Show your mind that you are not beaten. Convince your mind that you are going to succeed with positive actions by your body.

6. **Agility** – Be aware of who you are, what your strong and weak points are, what your goals are and where you are in your journey. This will help you to decide faster, adapt quicker and capitalize on opportunities, faster. Self-awareness can be the key to moving faster in a rapidly changing world.

7. **Bounce-Back** – The faster we recover after setbacks the stronger we become. One of the best ways to bounce-back is to have a bounce-back strategy in place. A strategy with steps like those in the list above will help you focus on what you should do next. It will help you to look past (not avoid) the emotional pain and get the gears of your life turning again.

Final thought: Being resilient means being aware of who you are, where you want to go and what price you are willing to pay to get there.

> " *I believe in process. I believe in four seasons.*
> *I believe that winter's tough, but spring's coming.*
> *I believe that there's a growing season.*
> *And I think that you realize that in life,*
> *you grow. You get better.* "
>
> **- Steve Southerland**

PREVENT BURNOUT

We live in a pressure cooker environment where we need to perform at the top of our ability, all the time. We are constantly under pressure to achieve and to be energetic. Unfortunately, this type of life is a breeding ground for depression and burnout. If we do not acknowledge this fact and actively take control of our lives, we will end up in a very deep hole, surrounded by regrets. No one is going to take responsibility for your life, for you and very few will understand when you end up burning out. Living your life on someone else's terms will bring you to the same catastrophic result.

> *Happiness cannot be travelled to, owned, earned, worn or consumed. Happiness is the spiritual experience of living every minute with love, grace, and gratitude.*
>
> **- Denis Waitley**

If we take control of our lives, we have a great chance of preventing burnout and the resulting regret. By taking control of our lives a host of benefits present themselves. Benefits like increased creativity, energy, inspiration, vision, insight, accurately interpreting situations, understanding people, seeing the big picture, being open to new ideas and many more.

How can we take control of our lives? I found an interesting article online, where they interviewed 13 entrepreneurs on their strategy to prevent burnout. They compiled a list of 13 action items from these interviews.

13 Action items to prevent burnout:

1. **Forget balance, find harmony** – Find a recipe that works for you and those closest to you.

2. **Know your breaking point** – Know yourself and understand what you need to function at your best.

3. **Fill your day with joy** – Do things that give you joy, every day. It can be small, just make sure you do it daily.

4. **Schedule free time** – Give yourself time to catch your breath and think about something else.

5. **Unplug** – Vacations and breakaways need to be away from work and not working away from the office.

6. **Travel and change your environment** – Work from a coffee shop or any place that gives you variation and inspiration.

7. **Pursue your passion** – Having a career that is also your passion, will get you out of bed easier in the morning.

8. **Take a nap** – Get enough sleep and plenty of rest. Give your body time to recover.

9. **Work out** – Exercise puts your body and mind in a good space.

10. **Live with mindfulness** – Being present in the moment and finding value right where you are will help you to find joy and cultivate happiness in your life.

11. **Find a hobby** – Do something else, something that gives you joy and something that energizes you.

12. **Build a great team** – A strong support structure will carry you through the good and the bad times.

13. Meditate daily – Your spirituality is part of your being, your reason for existence. Grant yourself enough time in that space.

Final thought: Many times, burnout is the result of us giving preference to the priorities of other people above our own. We don't have to storm in and change everything in our lives, but we can gradually introduce these action items to our lives. This will help us to cope better with challenges and find value in our lives.

> *" There is no passion to be found playing small - in settling for a life that is less than the one you are capable of living. "*
>
> **- Nelson Mandela**

MAKE CHANGE YOUR ALLY

We love consistency, the predictable and the planned. We love it when everything goes like clockwork. We love being in control and being the expert in the situation. We feel safe and secure, operating inside our comfort zones where we have the experience and where we know what will happen next. Unfortunately, the world is not revolving around the predictable. The mere fact that the world is revolving is one of the few things we can predict. The world requires more people who can operate outside their comfort zones. More people who can lead the way in a changing world with an uncertain future. People who can address the challenges of today by looking at tomorrow. We need people who can build a certain future out of an uncertain present.

> *Change your thoughts and you change your world.*
>
> **- Norman Vincent Peale**

Who are those people? They are probably not the ones walking in front, right now. They are the people that at this moment, are effectively dealing with change on a personal level. They are the people that are building extraordinary stories out of chaos. They are the people who can deal with the best with and adapt the best to change.

> *Every great dream begins with a dreamer.*
> *Always remember, you have within you*
> *the strength, patience, and the passion*
> *to reach for the stars to change the world.*
>
> **- Harriet Tubman**

We cannot prevent change, but we can make sure we deal with it in the best possible way. If you get Change right, Change can be the ally that catapults you to the front, the guide that gets you to the top.

10 Ways to make change your ally:

1. **Acknowledge and Accept** – Accept that change is a part of life. Understand that it does not matter what you think of change, change will happen anyway. Acknowledge change when it comes across your path so that you can use it to your advantage. Denying change will not make it go away. Tell yourself that change is going to make you, not break you. Know that change will bring exciting and wonderful things to your life even if you do not see it now. By accepting change, you are not disrespecting or forgetting what you had or where you came from. You are honouring what you had by using your experience and your past to build something beautiful.

2. **Schedule** – You cannot continue to do things the same way you used to. You are in a new chapter and you can create a fresh and different schedule. You have the opportunity to do fresh, exciting, and new things. Sticking to your old ways and your old schedule will bring you nowhere, you need to take control and adapt with your new chapter. Enjoy changing your schedule and make sure you put some great items in there.

3. **Communicate** – Talk to the right people about what is happening in your life. Tell them how you are experiencing it, what scares you and what excites you. Talk about your fears and your dreams so that you will be able to make sense in your mind, of your new environment. Listen to the advice of quality people and trusted advisors. Don't try to do it all on your own, allow people to lighten your load.

4. **Getaway** – Do enough things that you enjoy, things that renew your energy and motivation. Spend time on hobbies, breakaways, exercise and spend a lot of time with friends and loved ones. Build new memories.

5. **Design** – Set new goals and dream about new things. Start with small goals and milestones before moving onto the large ones. Find your feet before you start running. Make sure your new goals are relevant for your new journey and the place where you are now. Meet new people and talk about different things. Live life differently because you can.

6. **Your body** – Eat healthily, drink enough fluids, exercise regularly and take responsibility for your health. By taking care of your body you will get new energy and inspiration. Small, consistent steps are a sustainable approach.

7. **Emotional and Spiritual** – Give yourself time away from your daily life. Take time to rest and relax. Time to find new energy and inspiration. Do not neglect your faith or spirituality, you need to "connect". In other words, "Plugin when you are unplugged". Make sure you plug into a source that your soul hungers for, not a source someone else tells you to plugin to.

8. **Celebrate** – Find what you are grateful for and celebrate it. Celebrate your small steps forward. Celebrate the new future that awaits you. Celebrate life. Celebrate people. Celebrate, celebrate, celebrate...

9. **Depressurize** – You are playing on a new field and with new gear. Use what you have without putting too much pressure on yourself. Keep in mind that you still must find your feet. In time you will discover new resources and more effective ways of doing

things, but for now; Do what you can with what you have. Choose consistency above speed.

10. **Your story** – Even though you are in a new chapter, you are still writing your life's story. This is not a sub or inferior chapter. This is your new chapter and you need to be proud of it. Tell your story to yourself and find your inspiration and direction, there. When you find your inspiration in your story, share it with others. They need your story to help them make sense of theirs.

11. **Simplicity** – We adapt faster to change when we do not travel with loads of emotional and physical baggage. The key to successfully adapting to change is to travel light. Find ways to set yourself free of your emotional and physical baggage, so that you can live a full life as a complete human being in your new reality. Acknowledge your past, acknowledge what you had and the mistakes you made. Be grateful for your past, learn from it and use it effectively in your future. The precious people and the wonderful events of your past will always be in your heart to keep you company on your journey. Give away or sell things that you do not need. If you replace it, replace it with things that you need (physical and emotional). Do not clutter and complicate your life with things that you don't need.

Final thought: To be successful, you do not need to be the best, the most talented or the smartest. You just need to be able to adapt successfully. Let change show you something new and then show the world something new because you changed.

> *Sometimes if you want to see a change for the better, you have to take things into your own hands.*

- Clint Eastwood

UNLOCK YOUR INFLUENCE

Leadership is one of the ways we can shape the future. Unfortunately, leadership is a commodity that is in short supply. We desperately need more people to show the way and to lead the journey. We also need more leaders who are willing to develop more leaders. Leadership is a team sport and probably very close to a relay race. The core function of leadership is to make use of a very practical approach to develop more leaders. If this is not executed effectively there will be no one to pass the baton to.

The question beckons: why do we have so many so-called leaders and yet so little leadership?

One reason is that the leadership of our time don't have accountable influence. They don't understand the principles of leadership and they also don't understand people. Keep in mind that people are the main reason for leadership. Without people, leadership is an extinct trade in a dusty dictionary. We, therefore, need to expand our influence to become effective leaders.

> *Leadership is not about a title or a designation. It's about impact, influence and inspiration. Impact involves getting results, influence is about spreading the passion you have for your work, and you have to inspire team-mates and customers.*
>
> **- Robin S. Sharma**

Responsible and accountable Influence is one of the keys that unlock the unlimited potential of people. If we get it right, we can create a wonderful future and if we get it wrong, we destroy ourselves.

Nine principles to unlock your influence:

1. **Integrity** – One of the most valuable commodities in life is called, Integrity. Integrity shows that you can be trusted. To me, integrity is: What I say about you when you are in the room, I also say when you are not in the room. Integrity lays the foundation for any relationship.

2. **Trust** – If we don't trust people, we cannot have a deep-rooted relationship with them and we most definitely cannot influence them. Trust goes both ways but, in this case, we must trust those who we want to lead and influence. We need to trust them to take the baton from us and complete the race.

3. **Listen** – To be able to influence people we need to understand them. We need to make time to listen to them. Give them the opportunity to add value or just to share their personal experience or point of view.

4. **Hear** – Leadership and influence is not only about listening but more about hearing. Understanding the message that people are conveying to us. To hear is the ability to listen to and interpret what we hear so that we can put it to work to achieve a common goal.

5. **Lead** – Set the example and show the way so that people know where to go. All eyes are on you and you need to lead by example. Practical leadership means that you not only need to show that way, but you also need to help to build the road. The best place

to lead is on the ground with the people. This is where they live and learn.

6. **Team** – Teamwork is one of the secrets of leadership. In strong teams, we can observe, communicate, learn, do, fail and start over until we succeed. It is a safe space where we take responsibility for each other and where we succeed together. Teams are the place where leadership is cultivated.

7. **Care** – Only by caring about people, can we earn their trust, respect and in turn be able to influence them. Our hearts need to be in the right place or else people will see through the masquerade and walk away. We need to truly care about those we want to hand the baton to.

8. **Teach** – Be a teacher and transfer values, ideas, experience, and the secrets of life. Take responsibility to equip people for the journey ahead.

9. **Connect** – Bring people together. Create conversation, knowledge, and opportunities. Be the link that binds people, purpose, ideas, and vision.

Final thought: Accountable influence is true leadership in action.

> *Think twice before you speak, because your words and influence will plant the seed of either success or failure in the mind of another.*

- Napoleon Hill

FINAL THOUGHT

As we journey through life there are numerous concepts to keep in mind while striving for happiness, success, excellence, and an inspirational legacy. The following checklist is based on this book and will help you stay focussed on the next step while enjoying your journey.

1. Vision and insight lead to great goals.
2. Goals keep us moving forward through the chaos and uncertainty around us.
3. A plan to reach our goals helps us to take the next step en route to our goal.
4. Resilience helps us to become stronger, smarter, and focussed in the face of adversity.
5. Agility and adaptability make us relevant and engaged on our journey.
6. Consistency creates habits and momentum.
7. Patience ensures that we reach the finish line.
8. Habits cultivate a quality life and great memories.
9. Great memories inevitably lead to a wonderful legacy.
10. Synergy means we do not have to travel alone and together we are better.
11. Your uniqueness gives flavour to life. You have an inspired story to live.
12. Time is precious, use it wisely.

13. Celebrate and laugh abundantly. Life is a celebration.
14. You do not need to have all the answers in life as long as you have some great questions.
15. Never stop learning, experiencing, and growing. Evolve and become a better version of you.
16. You have a choice in the way you see life and the world. Choose your attitude wisely.
17. Never be afraid to lead but keep your followers close. Be prepared to follow a quality leader.
18. Failure is a growing experience. Do not avoid failure, learn from it.
19. Courage and fear go hand in hand.
20. Risk, creativity, and success are one family. Only those who risk can be creative and successful.
21. Great achievement comes from great sacrifice. Everything has a price.
22. Before you attempt anything, know if you are willing to pay the price for it.
23. Be unique and live life on your terms. You may just be saving someone's life.
24. Certain people will hate you and others will love you, no matter what you do.
25. Believe in yourself and your potential. You are worth the investment.
26. Find a unique balance in your life so that you have enough time for who and what you love.

27. Change might be the opportunity you have been waiting for. Make change your ally.

28. Keep moving; physically, emotionally, and spiritually.

29. Help people to become successful and you will be successful too.

30. Communication is the heart of success.

BIBLIOGRAPHY AND PREFERRED READING

Laurence, J Anthony. **Coming Back.** October 2018, Balboa Press, 1663 Liberty Drive Bloomington, IN 47403.

Maxwell, John C. **The 15 Invaluable Laws of Growth**. September 2012, Hachette Book Group Inc, New York.

Maxwell, John C. **The 21 Irrefutable laws of leadership.** 2007, Nelson Books, Nashville Tennessee.

Covey, Stephen R. **The Seven Habits of Highly Effective people**. 1994, Simon & Schuster Ltd, West Garden Place, Kendal Street, London.

Carnegie, Dale. **How to win friends and influence people.** Simon & Schuster Ltd, West Garden Place, Kendal Street, London.

Godin, Seth. **Purple Cow.** 2005, Penguin Books, New York.

Buford, Robert P. **Half Time.** 1994, Zondervan, Grand Rapids, Michigan.

Sinek, Simon. **Start with why.** 2009, Penguin Books, 375 Hudson Street, New York.

Maxwell, John C. **Becoming a Person of Influence.** 1997, Maxwell Motivation Inc, California.

Neethling, Kobus and Rachė Rutherford. **Creativity Uncovered**. 2014, Solutionsfinding, Menlo Park, Pretoria.

Putter, Jannie. **Mentally Tough.** 2012, Paarl Media, Jan van Riebeeck drive, Paarl, South Africa.

Voss, Chris. **Never Split the Difference.** 2016, HarperCollins Publishers, 195 Broadway, New York.

www.ingramcontent.com/pod-product-compliance
Lightning Source LLC
Chambersburg PA
CBHW071358290426
44108CB00014B/1605